Introduction

When I started freesciencelessons in 2013, I had one simple goal: to help students with their understanding of science. When I was at school (and we're talking thirty years ago now), science was always my favourite subject. It's not surprising that I went on to become a science teacher. I know that many students find science challenging. But I really believe that this doesn't have to be the case. With patient teaching and a bit of hard work, any student can make amazing progress.

Back in 2013, I had no idea how big freesciencelessons would become. The channel now has nearly 70 million views from 192 countries with a total view time of over 300 years. I love to hear from the students who have patiently watched the videos and realised that they can do science after all, despite in many cases having little confidence in their ability. And just like in 2013, I still make all the videos myself (many students think that I have a staff of helpers, but no, it's just me).

This workbook is designed to complement the Chemistry 2 videos for the AQA specification. However, there is a huge amount of overlap with other exam boards and in the future I'll be making videos and workbooks for those as well. I've packed the workbook full of questions to help you with your science learning. You might decide to start at the beginning and answer every question in the book or you might prefer to dip in and out of chapters depending on what you want to learn. Either way is fine. I've also written very detailed answers for every question, again to help you really develop your understanding. You can find these by scanning the QR code on the front of the book or by visiting freesciencelessons.co.uk/c2tv1

Please don't think of science as some sort of impossible mountain to climb. Yes there are some challenging bits but it's not as difficult as people think. Take your time, work hard and believe in yourself. When you find a topic difficult, don't give up. Just go to a different topic and come back to it later.

Finally, if you have any feedback on the workbooks, you're welcome to let me know (support@freesciencelessons.co.uk). I'm always keen to make the workbooks better so if you have a suggestion, I'd love to hear it.

Good luck on your journey. I hope that you get the grades that you want.

Shaun Donnelly

Revision Tips

The first important point about revision is that you need to be realistic about the amount of work that you need to do. Essentially you have to learn two years of work (or three if you start GCSEs in Year 9). That's a lot of stuff to learn. So give yourself plenty of time. If you're very serious about getting a top grade then I would recommend starting your revision as early as you can. I see a lot of messages on Youtube and Twitter from students who leave their revision until the last minute. That's their choice but I don't think it's a good way to get the best grades.

To revise successfully for any subject (but I believe particularly for science), you have to really get into it. You have to get your mind deep into the subject. That's because science has some difficult concepts that require thought and concentration. So you're right in the middle of that challenging topic and your phone pings. Your friend has sent you a message about something that he saw on Netflix. You reply and start revising again. Another message appears. This is from a different friend who has a meme they want to share. And so on and so on.

What I'm trying to tell you is that successful revision requires isolation. You need to shut yourself away from distractions and that includes your phone. Nothing that any of your friends have to say is so critically important that it cannot wait until you have finished. Just because your friends are bored does not mean that your revision has to suffer. Again, it's about you taking control.

Remember to give yourself breaks every now and then. You'll know when it's time. I don't agree with people who say you need a break every fifteen minutes (or whatever). Everyone is different and you might find that your work is going so well that you don't need a break. In that case don't take one. If you're taking breaks every ten minutes then the question I would ask is do you need them? Or are you trying to avoid work?

There are many different ways to revise and you have to find what works for you. I believe that active revision is the most effective. I know that many students like to copy out detailed notes (often from my videos). Personally, I don't believe that this is a great way to revise since it's not really active. A better way is to watch a video and then try to answer the questions from this book. If you can't, then you might want to watch the video again (or look carefully at the answers to check the part that you struggled with).

The human brain learns by repetition. So the more times that you go over a concept, the more fixed it will become in your brain. That's why revision needs so much time because you really need to go over everything more than once (ideally several times) before the exam.

Revision Tips

I find with my students that flashcards are a great way to learn facts. Again, that's because the brain learns by repetition. My students write a question on one side and the answer on the other. They then practise them until they've memorised the answer. I always advise them to start by memorising five cards and then gradually adding in extra cards, rather than try to memorise fifty cards at once.

I've noticed over the last few years that more students do past paper practise as a way of revising. I do not recommend this at all. A past paper is what you do AFTER you have revised. Imagine that you are trying to learn to play the guitar. So you buy a guitar and rather than having lessons, you book yourself into a concert hall to give a performance. And you keep giving performances until you can play. Would you recommend that as a good strategy? I wouldn't. But essentially that's how lots of students try to revise. Yes by all means do practise papers (I've included a specimen paper in this book for you) but do them at the end when you've done all your revision. Past papers require you to pull lots of different bits of the specification together, so you should only do them when you are capable of that (ie when you've already done loads of revision).

A couple of final points ....

To reduce our environmental impact and to keep the price of this book reasonable, the answers are available online. Simply scan the QR code on the front or visit www.freesciencelessons.co.uk/c2tv1

There will be times when I decide to update a book, for example to make something clearer or maybe to correct a problem (I hope not many of those). So please keep an eye out for updates. I'll post them on Twitter (@UKscienceguy) and also on the FAQ page of my website. If you think that you've spotted a mistake or a problem, please feel free to contact me.

Copyright information: The copyright of this workbook belongs to Shaun Donnelly. Copying of this workbook is strictly prohibited. Anyone found in breach of copyright will be prosecuted.

The Periodic Table of the Elements

1	2											3	4	5	6	7	0
						1 **H** hydrogen 1											4 **He** helium 2
7 **Li** lithium 3	9 **Be** beryllium 4											11 **B** boron 5	12 **C** carbon 6	14 **N** nitrogen 7	16 **O** oxygen 8	19 **F** fluorine 9	20 **Ne** neon 10
23 **Na** sodium 11	24 **Mg** magnesium 12											27 **Al** aluminium 13	28 **Si** silicon 14	31 **P** phosphorus 15	32 **S** sulfur 16	35.5 **Cl** chlorine 17	40 **Ar** argon 18
39 **K** potassium 19	40 **Ca** calcium 20	45 **Sc** scandium 21	48 **Ti** titanium 22	51 **V** vanadium 23	52 **Cr** chromium 24	55 **Mn** manganese 25	56 **Fe** iron 26	59 **Co** cobalt 27	59 **Ni** nickel 28	63.5 **Cu** copper 29	65 **Zn** zinc 30	70 **Ga** gallium 31	73 **Ge** germanium 32	75 **As** arsenic 33	79 **Se** selenium 34	80 **Br** bromine 35	84 **Kr** krypton 36
85 **Rb** rubidium 37	88 **Sr** strontium 38	89 **Y** yttrium 39	91 **Zr** zirconium 40	93 **Nb** niobium 41	96 **Mo** molybdenum 42	[98] **Tc** technetium 43	101 **Ru** ruthenium 44	103 **Rh** rhodium 45	106 **Pd** palladium 46	108 **Ag** silver 47	112 **Cd** cadmium 48	115 **In** indium 49	119 **Sn** tin 50	122 **Sb** antimony 51	128 **Te** tellurium 52	127 **I** iodine 53	131 **Xe** xenon 54
133 **Cs** caesium 55	137 **Ba** barium 56	139 **La*** lanthanum 57	178 **Hf** hafnium 72	181 **Ta** tantalum 73	184 **W** tungsten 74	186 **Re** rhenium 75	190 **Os** osmium 76	192 **Ir** iridium 77	195 **Pt** platinum 78	197 **Au** gold 79	201 **Hg** mercury 80	204 **Tl** thallium 81	207 **Pb** lead 82	209 **Bi** bismuth 83	[209] **Po** polonium 84	[210] **At** astatine 85	[222] **Rn** radon 86
[223] **Fr** francium 87	[226] **Ra** radium 88	[227] **Ac*** actinium 89	[261] **Rf** rutherfordium 104	[262] **Db** dubnium 105	[266] **Sg** seaborgium 106	[265] **Bh** bohrium 107	[277] **Hs** hassium 108	[268] **Mt** meitnerium 109	[271] **Ds** darmstadtium 110	[272] **Rg** roentgenium 111							

Contents

Contents

Contents

Contents

Contents

Chapter 1: Rates of Reaction

- Use the steepness of the slope of a graph to give an idea of the rate of reaction.
- Describe why the rate of reaction changes over time.
- Calculate the mean rate of a chemical reaction from a table or graph.
- Calculate the rate of a chemical reaction at a specific point by drawing a tangent.
- Describe the effect of concentration of reactant on the rate of a reaction in terms of the frequency of successful collisions.
- Describe how to determine the effect of concentration on the rate of reaction by using a method that involves a change in turbidity and a method that involves measuring the volume of a gas (required practical).
- Describe the effect of surface area on the rate of a chemical reaction in terms of the frequency of successful collisions.
- Describe what is meant by activation energy and how this effects the rate of a chemical reaction.
- Describe the effect of temperature on the rate of a chemical reaction in terms of activation energy and the frequency of successful collisions.
- Describe the effect of catalysts on the rate of a chemical reaction.
- Describe what is meant by a reversible reaction and by equilibrium.
- Describe the energy changes that take place in a reversible reaction.
- State Le Chatelier's principle.
- Use Le Chatelier's principle to describe the effect of concentration on reversible reactions at equilibrium.
- Use Le Chatelier's principle to describe the effect of temperature on reversible reactions at equilibrium.
- Use Le Chatelier's principle to describe the effect of pressure of gases on reversible reactions at equilibrium.

Mean Rate of a Chemical Reaction

1. In any chemical reaction the reactant forms the product.

If we plot the amount of product formed with time, we get the graph shown below.

a. Complete the following sentence by circling the correct answer.

> The steeper the slope of the curve, the faster / slower the reaction

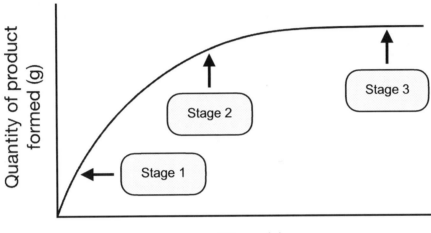

b. The boxes below describe what is happening in the graph above.

Decide whether each statement applies to stage 1, stage 2 or stage 3.

Only a small number of reactant molecules are reacting per second	Here all of the reactant has been used up	The reaction has stopped	The reaction is slowing down	The reaction is at its fastest

Here the amount of reactant is greatest	The maximum number of reactant molecules are reacting per second	Here the amount of reactant is running out	Because there is no reactant no more product forms

c. Now write each statement in the correct order below to describe what is happening at each stage.

2. We can calculate the mean rate of reaction using the equation on the right.

Remember that the units of rate are g / s or cm³ / s for a gas.

$$\text{Mean rate of reaction} = \frac{\text{Quantity of product formed}}{\text{Time taken}}$$

a. The equation below shows the reaction between magnesium and chlorine.

Magnesium   +   Chlorine   ⟶   Magnesium chloride

25 g of magnesium chloride was formed in 100 seconds. Calculate the mean rate of reaction.

b. The equation below shows the reaction that takes place when calcium carbonate is heated.

Calcium carbonate   —Heat→   Calcium oxide   +   Carbon dioxide

100 cm³ of carbon dioxide gas was formed in 200 seconds. Calculate the mean rate of reaction.

3. We can also calculate the mean rate of reaction from the quantity of reactant used.

The equation is shown on the right.

Again, remember that the units of rate are g / s or cm³ / s for a gas.

$$\text{Mean rate of reaction} = \frac{\text{Quantity of reactant used}}{\text{Time taken}}$$

a. The equation below shows the reaction between zinc and sulfuric acid.

Zinc   +   Sulfuric acid   ⟶   Zinc sulfate   +   Water

6 g of zinc was used in 18 seconds. Calculate the mean rate of reaction (to 2 significant figures).

b. The equation below shows the reaction between potassium and oxygen.

Potassium   +   oxygen   ⟶   Potassium oxide

80 cm³ of oxygen gas was used in 40 seconds. Calculate the mean rate of reaction.

4. We can also calculate the mean rate of reaction from a graph.

A scientist carried out a reaction to produce calcium chloride.

She measured the mass of calcium chloride produced every 10 seconds.

The results are shown below.

a. Determine the mean rate of reaction at 30 seconds. Give your answer to 2 significant figures.

b. Determine the time that the reaction had finished.

Explain why the reaction finished at that point.

5. You could also be expected to determine the mean rate of reaction in terms of moles.

In this case, the unit of rate is mol / s.

Link to Paper One
Calculating number of moles
is in Chemistry 1
Quantitative Chemistry

a. 21g of lithium were produced in 60 seconds.

Determine the mean rate of reaction. A_r Li = 7

b. 112g of ethene (C_2H_4) were produced in 40 seconds.

Determine the mean rate of reaction. A_r C = 12, A_r H = 1

Using Tangents to Determine Rate

1. As we saw in the previous topic, we can produce a graph showing how the quantity of product formed varies with the time of the reaction.

Complete the sentences below by using the correct words from the list.

tangent   less   changing   reactant   steep   used   slope

With any chemical reaction, the _____ of the line gives us an idea of the rate. Initially,

the graph shows a _____ slope, telling us that the rate is very rapid. This is because

there is a large amount of _____ molecules available to form the product. However,

after some time, the slope of the graph becomes _____ steep, telling us that the rate of

the reaction is not as rapid. This is because some of the reactant has been _____ up.

Because the rate is constantly _____ , it can be difficult to see the rate at any point.

To solve this, scientists draw a straight line to the curve. This is called a _____ .

2. The graph below shows the mass of product made in a chemical reaction.

Link the tangent on the graph with the correct description and explanation.

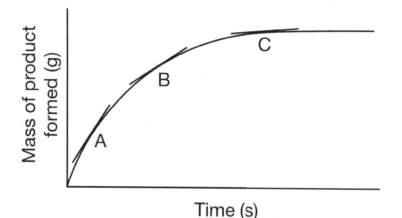

Time (s)

| A |

| The slope of this tangent is the least steep | | This is the greatest rate of reaction shown by the three tangents |

| B |

| This tangent has the steepest slope | | This is the slowest rate of reaction shown by the three tangents |

| C |

| The slope of this tangent is between the other two | | This rate of reaction is between the other two shown by the tangents |

3. A scientist carried out a reaction to produce oxygen gas (O_2).

The graph below shows how the volume of oxygen changes with time.

a. Draw a tangent to determine the rate of reaction at 30 seconds.

Give your answer to 2 significant figures.

Rate of reaction = _____ cm^3 / s

b. Draw a tangent to determine the rate of reaction at 60 seconds.

Give your answer to 2 significant figures.

Rate of reaction = _____ cm^3 / s

c. Explain why the two rates are different.

d. Using your answer to question 3a, calculate the rate of reaction in mol / s.

The volume of one mole of any gas is 24 dm^3 at room temperature and pressure.

Link to Paper One
Working with gas volumes is
in Chemistry 1
Quantitative Chemistry

Effect of Concentration of Reactants on Rate

1. The rate of a reaction is explained using collision theory.

a. Complete the sentences below by selecting the correct words from the boxes.

For a reaction to take place, the reacting particles must
> combine
> merge
> collide

with each other. If these have

sufficient
> electrons
> energy
> bonding

then the collision is successful and a reaction happens. The rate of the chemical

reaction is determined by the
> frequency
> number
> amount

of successful collisions.

b. What is the difference between "frequency" of successful collisions and "number" of successful collisions?

---

2. The diagrams below show three containers under identical conditions.

The containers contain two chemicals which can react.

a. Order the containers by the rate of reaction.

Explain your answer.

Container A

Container B

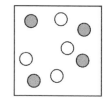
Container C

b. The graphs show the mass of product formed in a reaction using two concentrations of the reactants.

State two differences between the graphs and explain them using collision theory.

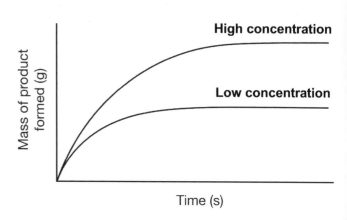

Required Practical: Rates of Reaction

1. In this required practical, you will be investigating the effect of concentration of the reactants on the rate of reaction.

As part of this practical, you are meant to develop a hypothesis.

a. Complete the sentences below.

A hypothesis is a proposal which could _____ a fact or an observation.

A key idea in science is that a hypothesis must be _____ .

b. Suggest a hypothesis for how the concentration of reactants affects the rate of a reaction.

2. One method of investigating the hypothesis is to use the disappearing cross experiment.

When we mix sodium thiosulfate and hydrochloric acid, the mixture turns cloudy.

The equation for this reaction is shown below.

Sodium thiosulfate   +   Hydrochloric acid   ⟶   Sulfur   +   Other products

a. Use the equation to explain why this reaction turns cloudy.

b. First we use a measuring cylinder to transfer 10cm³ of sodium thiosulfate into a clean conical flask.

Explain why we use a measuring cylinder to measure the volume of liquids.

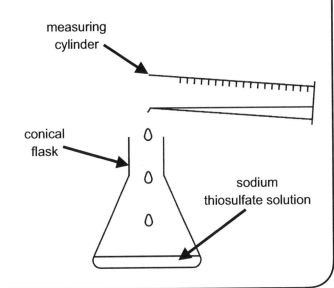

measuring cylinder

conical flask

sodium thiosulfate solution

c. Next we place the conical flask on to a printed black cross.

At the end of the practical, different groups can compare their results.

What is the advantage of using a printed black cross rather than a cross drawn by hand?

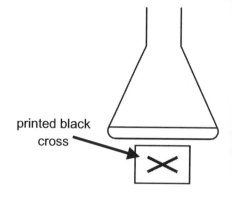

printed black cross

d. We then use a measuring cylinder to add 10cm³ of hydrochloric acid to the conical flask.

We then swirl the conical flask and start a stopwatch.

What is the purpose of swirling the conical flask?

e. At this point, we look down the conical flask to the black cross.

Over time, the solution will become cloudy.

We stop timing when the cross is no longer visible.

Explain why measuring the reaction in this way may make it difficult to compare results with different groups.

19.50

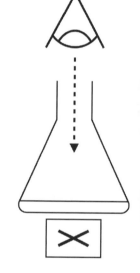

f. We then repeat the experiment with a lower concentration of sodium thiosulfate.

Write IV for the independent variable, DV for the dependent variable and CV for the control variables.

| person looking at the cross | temperature of the solutions | concentration of sodium thiosulfate solution | volume of hydrochloric acid |

| time for cross to no longer be visible | concentration of hydrochloric acid | volume of sodium thiosulfate solution |

. A student carried out the disappearing cross experiment.

Her results are shown below.

Concentration of sodium thiosulfate (mol / dm³)	Time for X to not be visible (s)			
	Repeat 1	Repeat 2	Repeat 3	Mean
0.25	17	21	25	21
0.20	38	30	34	34
0.15	48	44	87	
0.10	104	112	108	108

a. Calculate a mean value for 0.15 mol / dm³ sodium thiosulfate and write this in the table above.

b. Are the student's results repeatable?

Explain your answer.

c. Plot the values on the graph paper below and draw a line of best fit.

d. From these results, what is the effect of the concentration of reactant on the time taken for the cross to not be visible?

4. In this required practical, you could use a different method to investigate the effect of concentration on the rate of reaction.

This method involves measuring the volume of gas produced by a chemical reaction.

a. The stages are shown below.

Write a number next to each stage to place them in the correct order.

At this point, we add a 3 cm strip of magnesium to the acid. ⬜	The reaction produces hydrogen gas which will bubble into the measuring cylinder. ⬜
First we use a measuring cylinder to transfer 50 cm³ of hydrochloric acid into a conical flask. ⬜	When the reaction has stopped, we repeat the experiment using different concentrations of hydrochloric acid. ⬜
Now we replace the bung and start timing. ⬜	We now place the end of the delivery tube into the mouth of the measuring cylinder. ⬜
Place an upturned measuring cylinder into water so that the measuring cylinder is filled with water. ⬜	We then attach the conical flask to a bung and a delivery tube. ⬜
Every ten seconds we read the volume of hydrogen gas. ⬜	Continue taking readings until the reaction has stopped. ⬜

b. Label the diagram to show the equipment involved.

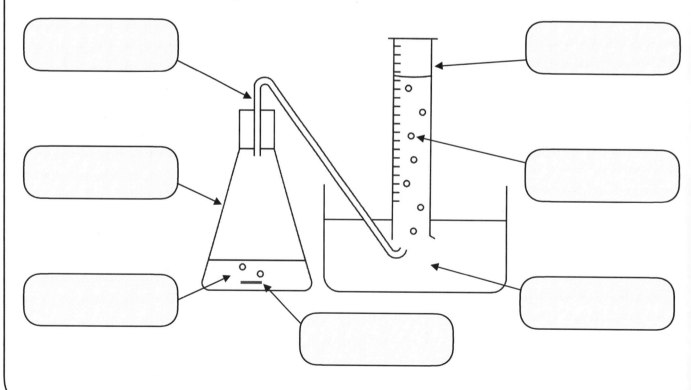

The graph below shows a student's results for this experiment.

c. Complete the graph by drawing a line of best fit for the higher concentration of hydrochloric acid.

d. Use tangents to calculate the rate of reaction at 20 seconds for the two concentrations.

Rate of reaction at higher concentration = _____ cm³ / s

Rate of reaction at lower concentration = _____ cm³ / s

e. If an investigation is carried out by a different person or by using different equipment or a different technique and the same results are obtained then the result is reproducible.

Are the results of the two experiments in this required practical reproducible?

Explain your answer.

Effect of Surface Area on Rate of Reaction

1. Calcium carbonate is a solid which reacts with hydrochloric acid.

The equation is shown below.

<table>
<tr><td>calcium
carbonate</td><td>+</td><td>hydrochloric
acid</td><td>→</td><td>calcium
chloride</td><td>+</td><td>carbon
dioxide</td><td>+</td><td>water</td></tr>
</table>

a. The diagrams below show calcium carbonate reacting with hydrochloric acid.

In each diagram, assume that the hydrochloric acid is the excess reactant.

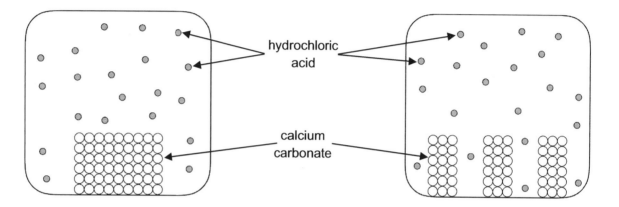

Colour the particles of calcium carbonate as follows:

- Blue for particles which can react with the hydrochloric acid.
- Red for particles which cannot react with the hydrochloric acid.

b. Complete the sentences below by selecting the correct words from the boxes.

If we take a solid and break it into smaller pieces, we have a

> smaller
> greater
> equal

rate of reaction.

This is because the smaller pieces have a

> equal
> smaller
> greater

surface area to volume ratio than the larger pieces.

Because of this, the

> frequency of
> number of
> total

successful collisions is greater with the smaller pieces.

c. In the diagram shown in question a, why will the final quantity of product be the same in both cases?

> The total amount of hydrochloric acid is the same in both cases

> The temperature is the same in both cases

> The total amount of calcium carbonate is the same in both cases

2. The diagrams below show three solid reactants and three graphs showing the quantity of product formed.

Link each diagram to the correct graph and explain your answer in each case.

Graph =

Graph =

Graph =

3. The following statements are true or false.

Circle true or false for each statement.

If the total mass is the same, smaller pieces of a solid will react faster than larger pieces.

TRUE / FALSE

Smaller pieces of a solid have a smaller surface area to volume ratio than larger pieces.

TRUE / FALSE

If the mass is the same, smaller pieces of solid will produce more product than larger pieces.

TRUE / FALSE

Smaller pieces of solid will have a greater frequency of collisions than larger pieces.

TRUE / FALSE

4. The reaction that we saw in question 1 produces carbon dioxide gas.

In the exam, you could be expected to describe the three ways to measure the quantity of gas produced.

The first two methods involve measuring the volume of carbon dioxide produced.

Method 1 - Using a measuring cylinder

carbon dioxide gas

measuring cylinder

Method 2 - Using a gas syringe

gas syringe

a. Describe two advantages of using a gas syringe compared to using a measuring cylinder.

b. When we use a measuring cylinder, the volume of carbon dioxide gas that we measure is often slightly less than if we use a gas syringe.

Which of the following could explain why?

The reaction makes more carbon dioxide using a gas syringe

Some of the carbon dioxide gas dissolves in the water

Some of the carbon dioxide escapes from the gas syringe

In the other method, we use a balance to determine the mass of carbon dioxide gas produced.

c. Describe the function of the cotton wool in this experiment.

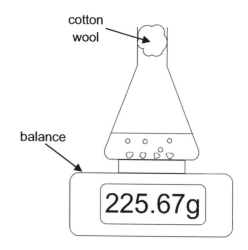

cotton wool

balance

225.67g

d. Why is it important to use a balance with a resolution of at least two decimal places?

e. One problem with all of these experiments is that the reaction can be too fast to measure accurately.

Suggest a way to overcome this problem.

Effect of Temperature on Rate of Reaction

1. The diagram shows the energy profile for a chemical reaction.

a. Explain how we can tell from the diagram that this reaction is exothermic.

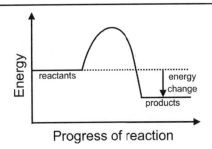

Energy

reactants

energy change

products

Progress of reaction

b. Complete the definition of activation energy below.

The activation energy is the minimum amount of _____ that the particles need in order to react (in other words to _____ successfully).

c. The diagram shows some particles in a gas.

The length of the arrows shows the energy of the particles.

The particles shown in the box labelled "A" have just enough energy to cross the activation energy barrier and collide successfully.

These particles will react.

Complete the boxes below to show what will happen to the particles shown by "B" and "C".

Particles in A

These have just enough energy to cross the activation energy barrier and react

Particles in B

Particles in C

2. The graph on the right shows the effect of temperature on a chemical reaction.

A fixed mass of chemical was reacted at three different temperatures.

a. Order the letters to show which reaction took place at which temperature. Explain your answer.

Low temperature ⟶ High temperature

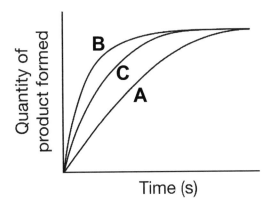

Quantity of product formed

B

C

A

Time (s)

b. Apart from activation energy, how else does a higher temperature increase the rate of chemical reactions?

At higher temperatures, the particles have less energy

At higher temperatures, there are more reacting particles

At higher temperatures, the frequency of collisions increases

Catalysts

1. Catalysts can play a really important role in chemical reactions.

a. Complete the sentences below by using the correct words from the list.

money   **pathway**   **used up**   **barrier**   **activation**   **collide**   **temperature**   **energy**

For a chemical reaction to occur, the particles must collide with a certain amount of _____.

Scientists call this the _____ energy. Catalysts increase the rate of chemical reactions by

providing a different _____ with a lower activation energy _____ . This

means that particles require less energy to _____ successfully and react. Catalysts are

not _____ during the reaction and can be reused. By using a catalyst, we can make a

reaction faster without increasing the _____ . This saves energy and _____ .

b. The diagrams below show the reaction profiles for an exothermic and endothermic reaction.
Complete the diagrams by showing the effect of a catalyst on the activation energy.

Exothermic reaction

Endothermic reaction

2. Nitrogen and hydrogen can be reacted to produce ammonia. Iron is used as a catalyst in this reaction.

Nitrogen   +   Hydrogen   +   Iron   Ammonia

a. Explain why this is not the correct way to show a catalyst in a chemical reaction.

b. Why can iron not be used as a catalyst in all chemical reactions?

c. What do scientists call catalysts found in living organisms?

| Hormones | Synapses | Enzymes |

Reversible Reactions

1. Two different chemical reactions are shown below.

a. Complete the boxes below each reaction to show what is happening in each case.

sodium + bromine ⟶ sodium bromide

ammonium chloride ⇌ (heat / cool) ammonia + hydrogen chloride

The arrow tells us that this is a reversible / non reversible reaction.

The products can / cannot go back and reform the reactants.

The arrow tells us that this is a reversible / non reversible reaction.

The products can / cannot go back and reform the reactants.

b. For the reaction on the right, describe what happens to the direction of the reaction if we change the conditions.

Heat the reaction

Reaction moves forwards / backwards

Cool the reaction

Reaction moves forwards / backwards

2. Many reversible reactions involve energy changes.

Hydrated copper sulfate contains water molecules trapped in the crystal.

When we heat hydrated copper sulfate, the following reaction takes place.

hydrated copper sulfate (blue) ⇌ (heat) anhydrous copper sulfate (white) + water

a. Explain how we know that the forward reaction is endothermic.

b. Describe what happens if we add water back to the anhydrous copper sulfate. Explain your answer.

c. Which of the boxes below best describes the energy changes in the above reaction?

The forward reaction takes in more energy than the reverse reaction releases

The forward reaction takes in less energy than the reverse reaction releases

The forward reaction takes in the same amount of energy as the reverse reaction releases

3. In a sealed container, a reversible reaction will reach equilibrium.

What can we say about the rates of the forward and reverse reactions at equilibrium?

Concentration and Reversible Reactions

1. Complete the following sentences by selecting the correct words from the boxes.

If we carry out a reversible reaction in a sealed container, none of the reactants or products can

change
react
escape

.

The reaction has reached

equalisation
equilibrium
equivalence

. At this point, the rate of the forward reaction will be

the same as
faster than
slower than

the reverse reaction. Now the concentrations of reactants and products will not change.

2. Le Chatelier's principle tells us what can happen when we make a change to a reversible reaction.

> If a system (reaction) is at equilibrium and we make a change to the conditions, the system (reaction) responds to counteract the change.

a. The equation below shows a reversible reaction. The reaction has reached equilibrium.

carboxylic acid   +   alcohol ester   +   water

Use Le Chatelier's principle to describe what would happen if we did the following.

Increasing the concentration of ester	Decreasing the concentration of water
Position of the equilibrium shifts to the left / right	Position of the equilibrium shifts to the left / right

Increasing the concentration of alcohol	Decreasing the concentration of carboxylic acid
Position of the equilibrium shifts to the left / right	Position of the equilibrium shifts to the left / right

b. Use Le Chatelier's principle to describe what happens to the equilibrium in the following reactions.

$2 NO_2 \rightleftharpoons N_2O_4$

Adding extra N_2O_4	Removing N_2O_4

$H_2 + Cl_2 \rightleftharpoons 2 HCl$

Removing HCl	Adding extra Cl_2

Temperature and Reversible Reactions

1. The reaction to produce ammonia is a reversible reaction.

The equation and energy profile for this reaction are shown.

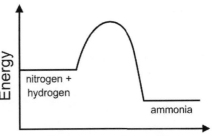

Nitrogen	Hydrogen	Ammonia
N_2 +	$3 H_2$ $\rightleftharpoons$	$2 NH_3$

a. Explain how the energy profile shows that this reaction is exothermic.

b. Use Le Chatelier's principle to describe what will happen to the equilibrium under the following conditions.

Increasing the temperature will shift the equilibrium to the left / right.

The reaction will release / take in energy.

This will cause the temperature to increase / decrease.

Decreasing the temperature will shift the equilibrium to the left / right.

The reaction will release / take in energy.

This will cause the temperature to increase / decrease.

2. The following reaction is used to make hydrogen iodide.

$$H_2 + I_2 \rightleftharpoons 2 HI$$

A scientist found that when she warmed the reaction, the equilibrium shifted to the right hand side.

Is the forward reaction exothermic or endothermic? Use Le Chatelier's principle to explain your answer.

3. The reaction shown below is exothermic in the forward direction.

$$2 NO_2 \rightleftharpoons N_2O_4$$

(brown)   (colourless)

Describe what will happen to the colour of the chemicals under the following conditions.

Explain your answer in each case.

Increase the reaction temperature

Decrease the reaction temperature

Pressure and Reversible Reactions

1. The diagram below shows four containers containing gas particles under identical conditions.

Highest pressure

a. Place the containers in order of pressure on the arrow on the right.

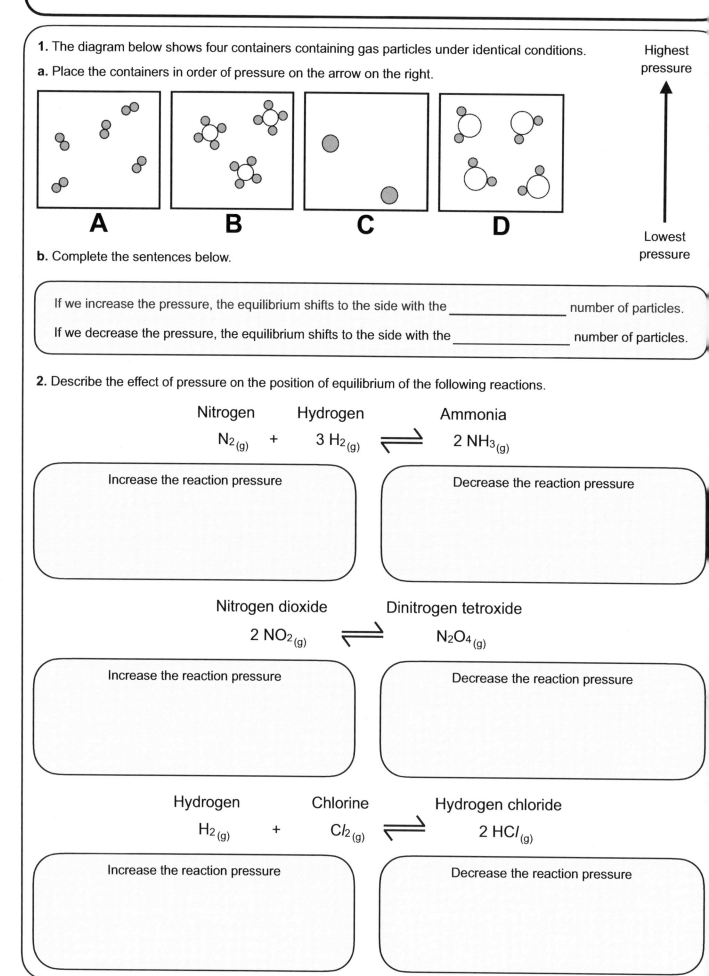

A   B   C   D

Lowest pressure

b. Complete the sentences below.

If we increase the pressure, the equilibrium shifts to the side with the _____ number of particles.

If we decrease the pressure, the equilibrium shifts to the side with the _____ number of particles.

2. Describe the effect of pressure on the position of equilibrium of the following reactions.

Nitrogen   Hydrogen   Ammonia

$$N_{2(g)} \quad + \quad 3\,H_{2(g)} \rightleftharpoons 2\,NH_{3(g)}$$

Increase the reaction pressure	Decrease the reaction pressure

Nitrogen dioxide   Dinitrogen tetroxide

$$2\,NO_{2(g)} \rightleftharpoons N_2O_{4(g)}$$

Increase the reaction pressure	Decrease the reaction pressure

Hydrogen   Chlorine   Hydrogen chloride

$$H_{2(g)} \quad + \quad Cl_{2(g)} \rightleftharpoons 2\,HCl_{(g)}$$

Increase the reaction pressure	Decrease the reaction pressure

Chapter 2: Organic Chemistry

- Describe what is meant by crude oil and how crude oil is formed.

- Describe what is meant by a hydrocarbon.

- Describe what is meant by an alkane and state the general formula for alkanes.

- Draw the structures of the alkanes methane, ethane, propane and butane.

- Describe how the viscosity, flammability and boiling point of the alkanes change with the length of the carbon chain.

- Write balanced equations for the complete combustion of hydrocarbons.

- Describe how the hydrocarbons in crude oil are separated by fractional distillation.

- Describe why long chain hydrocarbons are cracked.

- Describe the conditions for catalytic cracking and steam cracking.

- Balance cracking equations.

- Describe what is meant by an alkene and state the general formula for alkenes.

- Describe how to test for the presence of alkenes.

- Draw the structures of ethene, propene, butene and pentene.

- Describe the reactions of alkenes with hydrogen, water (steam) and halogens.

- Recognise the alcohol functional group and draw the structures of methanol, ethanol, propanol and butanol.

- Describe how ethanol can be made by hydration of ethene and fermentation of sugars.

- Describe what happens when alcohols are added to water, combusted or reacted with sodium or an oxidising agent.

- Recognise the carboxylic acid functional group.

- Explain why carboxylic acids are weak acids.

- Describe how carboxylic acids react with metal carbonates and alcohols.

- Describe the structures of addition polymers and condensation polymers.

- Describe the structure of DNA and other naturally occurring polymers.

Crude Oil and Hydrocarbons

Exam tip: Remember that you could be asked to demonstrate some knowledge from Paper 1 topics in your Paper 2 exam. We cover some of that in this section.

1. Which of the following products are made using crude oil?

Circle the correct products.

(Paper)　(Cosmetics)　(Petrol and diesel)　(Glass)　(Pharmaceuticals)　(Plastics)

2. Complete the sentences below by using the correct words from the list.

millions　　run out　　plankton　　finite　　hydrocarbons　　rocks　　mud　　sea　　carbon

Crude oil is found in _____ . Crude oil is described as a _____ resource.

This means that if we keep using it, crude oil will one day _____ . Crude oil is formed

from the remains of _____ , which are tiny creatures found in the _____

These were buried in _____ and formed crude oil over _____ of years.

Crude oil is a mixture of chemicals called _____ . These contain only the elements

hydrogen and _____ .

3. The diagram below shows the structures of ethane and ethanol.

Circle the correct word to show whether each molecule is a hydrocarbon.

Explain your answer below.

$$H-\overset{\overset{\displaystyle H}{|}}{\underset{\underset{\displaystyle H}{|}}{C}}-\overset{\overset{\displaystyle H}{|}}{\underset{\underset{\displaystyle H}{|}}{C}}-H$$

Ethane

Hydrocarbon Yes / No

$$H-\overset{\overset{\displaystyle H}{|}}{\underset{\underset{\displaystyle H}{|}}{C}}-\overset{\overset{\displaystyle H}{|}}{\underset{\underset{\displaystyle H}{|}}{C}}-O-H$$

Ethanol

Hydrocarbon Yes / No

4. The general formula allows us to work out the formula of any alkane.

a. What is the general formula for alkanes?

Circle the correct answer.

C_nH_{2n}

C_nH_{2n-2}

C_nH_{2n+2}

b. Use the general formula to work out the number of hydrogen atoms and the formulas of the following alkanes.

Name	Number of carbon atoms	Number of hydrogen atoms	Formula
Hexane	6		
Nonane	9		
Decane	10		
Dodecane	12		

5. Methane has the formula CH_4.

a. What does the formula CH_4 tell you about the atoms in a molecule of methane?

Link to Paper One
Covalent bonding is in
Chemistry 1
Structure and Bonding

b. Complete the dot and cross diagram below to show the covalent bonding in methane.

Carbon atoms have four outer electrons and hydrogen atoms have one outer electron.

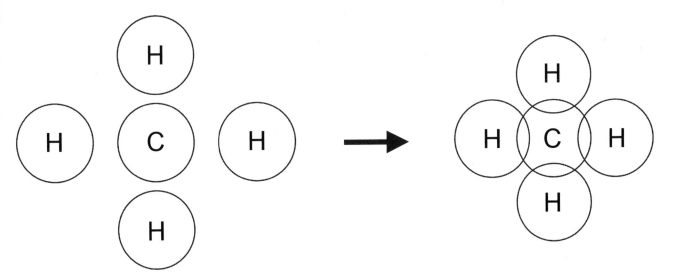

c. Carbon atoms always form four covalent bonds and hydrogen atoms always form one.

Use the idea of outer electrons to explain why.

6. Molecular models of the first four alkanes are shown below.

a. Write the name and formula for each alkane and draw the structure (methane has been done for you).

Name = methane

Formula = CH₄

$$H-\underset{\displaystyle H}{\overset{\displaystyle H}{C}}-H$$

b. What kind of chemical bonding is found in hydrocarbons?

Label one of these bonds in your diagrams above.

Properties of Hydrocarbons

. Viscosity tells us how quickly a liquid flows.

. The diagram shows a viscometer. These are used to measure viscosity.

The liquid is poured into the viscometer and timed to see how quickly it flows out.

Viscous liquids take a longer time than less viscous liquids.

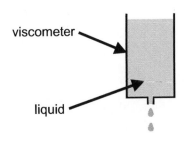

viscometer

liquid

Which of the following explains why the first four hydrocarbons (methane, ethane, propane and butane) cannot be used in a viscometer?

| They are solids at room temperature | They are gases at room temperature | They are too viscous |

b. Order the hydrocarbons below from least viscous to most viscous. Explain your answer.

$C_{15}H_{32}$

Order =

C_8H_{18}

Order =

$C_{20}H_{42}$

Order =

2. Another property of hydrocarbons is flammability.

a. What is meant by flammability?

b. How does the flammability change as we increase the length of the hydrocarbon chain?

3. The graph shows how the boiling points of the alkanes changes as the number of carbon atoms increases.

a. Draw a line of best fit through the points.

b. Use the graph to predict the boiling point of the alkane with 5 carbon atoms.

c. Room temperature is around 20°C.

Which alkanes on the graph are gases at room temperature?

Explain your answer.

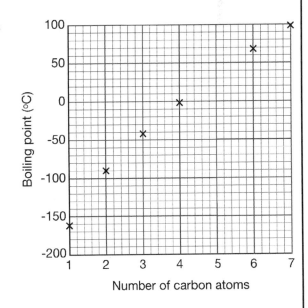

d. Which of the following best explains why the boiling point of the alkanes increases as the number of carbon atoms increases?

| The strength of the covalent bonds increases | The strength of the intermolecular forces decreases | The strength of the intermolecular forces increases |

Link to Paper One
Properties of small covalent molecules is in Chemistry 1 Structure and Bonding

Combustion of Hydrocarbons

1. Hydrocarbons make excellent fuels.

When they are combusted (burned), they release a lot of energy.

a. During combustion, hydrocarbons are oxidised. What does this mean?

b. When hydrocarbons are combusted in unlimited oxygen, they undergo complete combustion.

Which two chemicals are produced in complete combustion?

2. The following equations show the complete combustion of a hydrocarbon.

a. Balance each equation.

pentane	+	oxygen	$\longrightarrow$	carbon dioxide	+	water
C_5H_{12}	+	O_2		CO_2	+	H_2O

octane	+	oxygen	$\longrightarrow$	carbon dioxide	+	water
C_8H_{18}	+	O_2		CO_2	+	H_2O

b. From their formulas, how can we tell that the hydrocarbons in question 2a are both alkanes?

3. Write balanced equations for the following word equations.

methane	+	oxygen	$\longrightarrow$	carbon dioxide	+	water

propane	+	oxygen	$\longrightarrow$	carbon dioxide	+	water

Fractional Distillation of Crude Oil

Exam tip: You need to learn the stages of fractional distillation as it could be a six mark question. You also need to understand why hydrocarbons separate at different temperatures.

1. Some of the statements below are true and some are false.

Write a T next to the statements that are true and an F next to the statements that are false.

Crude oil is a mixture of molecules called hydrocarbons	Each hydrocarbon has the same boiling point	Each hydrocarbon has a different boiling point
Shorter chain hydrocarbons have a higher boiling point than longer chains	Longer chain hydrocarbons have a higher boiling point than shorter chains	Crude oil is a mixture of molecules called carbohydrates

2. Complete the sentences below by selecting the correct words from the boxes.

Crude oil is separated by
> paper chromatography
> crystallisation
> fractional distillation

. The crude oil is separated into fractions containing a

number of different hydrocarbons. Each hydrocarbon has a similar number of
> nitrogen
> carbon
> oxygen

atoms.

Fractional distillation works because the
> boiling
> melting
> freezing

point of each hydrocarbon is different.

3. The hydrocarbon fractions produced by fractional distillation have a number of uses.

a. Give two examples of hydrocarbon fractions that are used as fuels.

b. Some fractions are used as feedstock for the chemical industry.

Describe what is meant by the word "feedstock".

4. The diagram below shows a fractionating column used in fractional distillation.

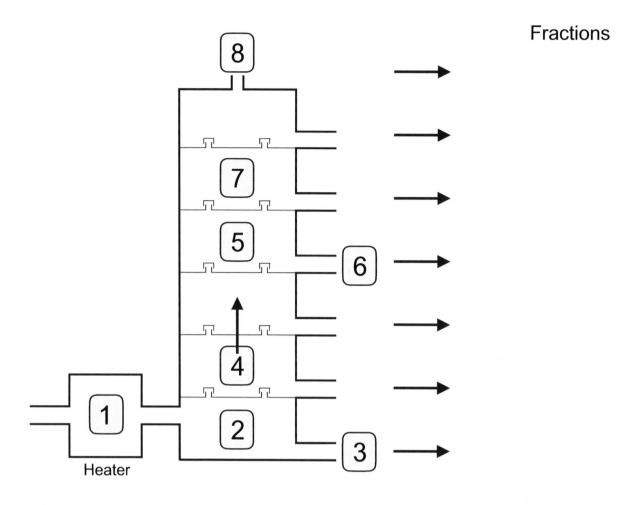

The numbers show the order of the stages in fractional distillation.

Match the statements below with the correct stage on the diagram.

Two have been done for you.

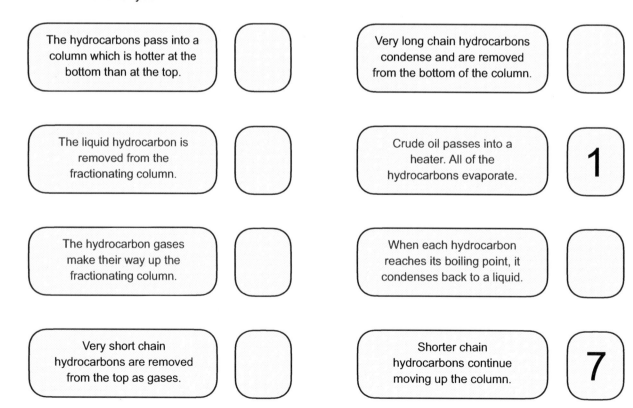

The hydrocarbons pass into a column which is hotter at the bottom than at the top.

Very long chain hydrocarbons condense and are removed from the bottom of the column.

The liquid hydrocarbon is removed from the fractionating column.

Crude oil passes into a heater. All of the hydrocarbons evaporate.   1

The hydrocarbon gases make their way up the fractionating column.

When each hydrocarbon reaches its boiling point, it condenses back to a liquid.

Very short chain hydrocarbons are removed from the top as gases.

Shorter chain hydrocarbons continue moving up the column.   7

. Different fractions are collected at different points on the fractionating column.

. Describe how the temperature of the column changes from the bottom to the top.

The table below shows the range of boiling points of some of the fractions.

Fraction	Approximate boiling point range (^{o}C)
Refinery gases	<25
Petrol	30-100
Naphtha	100-180
Kerosene	180-250
Diesel	250-350
Fuel oil	350-450
Bitumen	>500

b. Write the fractions in the correct places on the diagram on the previous page.

c. Which of the fractions above will have hydrocarbons with the greatest number of carbon atoms?

Explain your answer.

d. Explain why very short chain hydrocarbons are removed as gases rather than liquids.

e. Suggest why the boiling points are given as ranges rather than specific values.

f. Dodecane is a hydrocarbon found in crude oil. The boiling point of dodecane is 216°C.

Which fraction will dodecane be found in?

g. The kerosene fraction contains the hydrocarbon decane.

Kerosene is used as a fuel for airplanes.

Balance the equation below to show the complete combustion of decane.

decane	+	oxygen	$\longrightarrow$	carbon dioxide	+	water
$C_{10}H_{22}$	+	O_2		CO_2	+	H_2O

Cracking

1. The diagram below shows the structure of the alkane propane.

Number of carbon atoms = ⬚

Number of hydrogen atoms = ⬚

a. Complete the diagram to show the number of carbon atoms and hydrogen atoms in a molecule of propane.

b. Using your answer to part a, how do we know that the general formula of an alkane is C_nH_{2n+2}?

c. What type of covalent bonds do we find between the carbon atoms in alkanes?

Circle the correct answer.

single   **double**   **triple**

2. We use cracking to convert long chain hydrocarbons into shorter chain hydrocarbons to use as fuels.

a. Which of the following explains why we crack long chain hydrocarbons?

Long chain hydrocarbons are more flammable than short chain hydrocarbons

Long chain hydrocarbons are more expensive than short chain hydrocarbons

Long chain hydrocarbons are less flammable than short chain hydrocarbons

The diagram below shows the cracking of an alkane.

long chain alkane   ⟶   shorter chain alkane   +   alkene

b. Fill in the boxes to show the conditions for catalytic cracking and for steam cracking.

catalytic cracking

steam cracking

c. Describe a use of the alkene molecule produced in cracking.

d. Describe two ways that an alkene molecule is different from an alkane molecule.

. Alkenes are more reactive than alkanes.

We can test for alkenes by their reaction with bromine water.

. Complete the diagram below to show the colour change when an alkene is present.

bromine water ——— alkene ———▶ bromine water
(orange)   (...........................)

. Which of the following molecules would turn bromine water from orange to colourless?

Explain your answer.

4. In the exam, you could be asked to complete a cracking equation.

a. In the example below, draw the structure of the missing product.

b. In the examples below, write the formulas of the missing molecules.

$C_{30}H_{62}$ ———▶ $C_{25}H_{52}$ + ...

$C_{28}H_{58}$ ———▶ .... + $C_{10}H_{20}$

.... ———▶ $C_{14}H_{30}$ + C_6H_{12}

c. Explain how the formula tells us that $C_{30}H_{62}$ is an alkane.

d. Complete the following cracking equation (this one is more tricky).

$C_{40}H_{82}$ ———▶ $C_{32}H_{66}$ + 2 C......H......

Alkenes

1. Ethene is an example of an alkene.

Ethene has the molecular formula C_2H_4.

a. Draw the displayed formula of ethene in the space on the right.

b. Alkenes have at least one double bond between the carbon atoms.

Explain why there is no alkene called methene.

Displayed formula of ethene

c. Use the structure of ethene above to show that alkenes have the general formula C_nH_{2n}.

---

2. The molecular formulas and displayed formulas of propane, butane and pentane are shown below.

a. Next to each alkane, write the molecular formula and the displayed formula of the equivalent alkene.

Remember that at GCSE, the double bond can be between any of the carbon atoms.

```
      H   H   H
      |   |   |
  H — C — C — C — H                    ———————▶
      |   |   |
      H   H   H
      propane C₃H₈
```

```
      H   H   H   H
      |   |   |   |
  H — C — C — C — C — H                ———————▶
      |   |   |   |
      H   H   H   H
       butane C₄H₁₀
```

```
    H   H   H   H   H
    |   |   |   |   |
  H — C — C — C — C — C — H            ———————▶
    |   |   |   |   |
    H   H   H   H   H
        pentane C₅H₁₂
```

b. Unsaturated hydrocarbons have 2 fewer hydrogen atoms than the alkane with the same number of carbon atoms.

Using your answers to question 2a, show that the alkenes above are unsaturated.

Reactions of Alkenes 1

1. Complete the sentences below by using the correct words from the list.

two   reacts   similar   functional   covalent   one   homologous   same

Alkene molecules all react in a _____ way. This is because alkenes have a double

_____ bond between the carbon atoms. Scientists call the double bond the alkene

_____ group. The functional group is the part of the molecule that determines how the

molecule _____ . All of the alkenes have the _____ functional group.

Molecules that have the same functional group form a _____ series. All the molecules

in a homologous series have _____ extra carbon atom and _____

extra atoms of hydrogen.

2. The diagrams below show the alkenes propene and butene.

propene   butene

Complete the boxes to show how we can tell that both of these molecules are part of the same homologous series.

The functional group	The number of carbon and hydrogen atoms

3. The incomplete combustion of butene is shown below.

butene   +   oxygen   ⟶   carbon dioxide   +   water   +   carbon

C_4H_8 + O_2 CO_2 + H_2O +   2 C

a. Balance the above equation.

b. Use the equation to explain why alkenes tend to burn with a smoky flame.

4. The diagram below shows the reaction between the alkene ethene and hydrogen.

$$\underset{\text{ethene}}{\overset{H\quad H}{\underset{H\quad H}{C=C}}} \quad + \quad H_2 \quad \longrightarrow$$

a. Complete the diagram to show the product of this reaction.

b. Complete the sentences below by selecting the correct words from the boxes.

Reacting alkenes with hydrogen is called | dehydration / hydrogenation / hydration | . The conditions for this reaction are

using a | copper / manganese / nickel | catalyst and a temperature of around | 15°C / 150°C / 1500°C | .

> **Link to Paper One**
> Transition metals is in
> Chemistry 1 Atomic Structure
> and the Periodic Table

c. Complete the diagrams to show the products when the following alkenes are reacted with hydrogen.

$$\underset{\text{propene}}{\overset{H\quad H\quad H}{\underset{H\qquad H}{C=C-C-H}}} \quad + \quad H_2 \quad \longrightarrow$$

$$\underset{\text{butene}}{\overset{H\quad H\quad H\quad H}{\underset{H\qquad H\quad H}{C=C-C-C-H}}} \quad + \quad H_2 \quad \longrightarrow$$

$$\underset{\text{pentene}}{\overset{H\quad H\quad H\quad H\quad H}{\underset{H\qquad H\quad H\quad H}{C=C-C-C-C-H}}} \quad + \quad H_2 \quad \longrightarrow$$

d. Which type of molecule is produced when an alkene is reacted with hydrogen?

| Alcohol | Alkane | Carboxylic acid |

Reactions of Alkenes 2

1. The alkenes form a homologous series.

a. Which of the following best describes a homologous series?

Molecules with the same functional group but with an additional hydrogen atom and two carbon atoms

Molecules with a different functional group and with an additional carbon atom and two hydrogen atoms

Molecules with the same functional group but with an additional carbon atom and two hydrogen atoms

b. Why do the different alkenes all react in a similar way?

2. We can react alkenes with water in the form of steam.

This is shown for ethene below.

ethene	steam	

Conditions =

Catalyst =

Product = ...

a. Write in the name of the product of this reaction.

b. Write the conditions and the catalyst required for this reaction.

c. What name do scientists give to this type of reaction?

d. This reaction is reversible. How do scientists increase the yield of the ethanol produced?

e. The hydration of butene is shown below. Complete the diagram to show the product.

butene   steam

300ºC
70 atmospheres
pressure

phosphoric acid
catalyst

f. Use Le Chatelier's principle to explain why hydration takes place at a high pressure (clue: all of the reactants and products are gases in the conditions of the reaction).

3. We can also react alkenes with halogens (elements from group 7).

a. The diagrams below show the reactions between three alkenes and different halogens.

In each case, name the product molecule and draw its structure.

ethene   + Cl_2 ⟶

propene   + Br_2 ⟶

butene   + I_2 ⟶

The diagram below shows the molecule produced when an alkene is reacted with a halogen.

b. Write the name of the molecule produced.

c. Draw the original alkene in the space below.

+ Br_2 ⟶

name = ...

Alcohols

1. Alcohols are very important molecules in Chemistry.

a. State three uses of alcohols.

b. The displayed formula and structural formula of methanol are shown below.

Label the alcohol functional group on both diagrams.

c. The displayed formula of ethanol and propanol are shown below.

Use the displayed formula to determine the structural formula for each molecule and write these in the spaces.

Structural formula

Structural formula

d. The structural formula of butanol is shown below.

Use the structural formula to draw the displayed formula of butanol.

$CH_3CH_2CH_2CH_2OH$

e. Explain why all of the alcohols are part of a homologous series.

2. We can make alcohols using two different methods.

The first method is hydration, which we saw on page 45.

The second method is fermentation of a sugar (such as glucose). Fermentation is shown below.

$$\text{glucose} \xrightarrow[\text{30°C}]{\text{yeast}} \text{ethanol} \; + \; \text{carbon dioxide}$$

a. In order to make ethanol, fermentation must be carried out in anaerobic conditions.

What is meant by anaerobic conditions?

b. Both hydration and fermentation have advantages and disadvantages. These are shown in the statements below.

Complete the table by writing each statement under the correct heading.

Write "A" if the statement is an advantage and "D" if the statement is a disadvantage.

Hydration	Advantage / Disadvantage	Fermentation	Advantage / Disadvantage

This reaction produces a high yield of ethanol.	This reaction requires a high temperature, needing a lot of energy.	The starting material comes from plants and is therefore renewable.	This reaction can only be used to make the alcohol ethanol.
This makes an aqueous solution of ethanol. Distilling the ethanol requires energy.	This reaction requires a low temperature so not much energy is needed.	This reaction can produce any alcohol not just ethanol.	The starting material comes from crude oil and is non renewable.

Reactions of Alcohols

---

1. We can dissolve alcohols in water.

a. What colour will universal indicator turn if placed in a solution of alcohol in water?

Explain your answer.

b. Order the following alcohols in order of solubility: methanol, ethanol, propanol, butanol.

Least
soluble
$\xrightarrow{\hspace{6cm}}$
Most
soluble

---

2. Alcohols react with sodium.

The equation for the reaction of ethanol is shown below.

$$2\ C_2H_5OH_{(l)} \quad + \quad 2\ Na_{(s)} \quad \longrightarrow \quad 2\ C_2H_5ONa_{(l)} \quad + \quad H_{2(g)}$$

ethanol   sodium   sodium ethoxide   hydrogen

a. What would you see if you carried out this reaction?

Explain your answer.

b. Complete the equation below for the reaction between propanol and sodium.

$$2\ C_3H_7OH_{(l)} \quad + \quad 2\ Na_{(s)} \quad \longrightarrow$$

propanol   sodium

---

3. When alcohols react with an oxidising agent, they produce a carboxylic acid.

The reaction between butanol and an oxidising agent is shown below.

a. Complete the diagram to show the structural formula of the carboxylic acid produced.

$$CH_3CH_2CH_2CH_2OH \ + \ \overset{\text{oxidising}}{\underset{\text{agent}}{}} \longrightarrow \qquad\qquad + \ H_2O$$

The reaction below shows the production of a carboxylic acid.

b. Write the structural formula of the alcohol used to produce this.

$$+ \ \overset{\text{oxidising}}{\underset{\text{agent}}{}} \longrightarrow \ CH_3CH_2COOH \ + \ H_2O$$

---

4. Balance the equations below to show the combustion of two different alcohols.

$$C_2H_5OH \quad + \quad O_2 \quad \longrightarrow \quad CO_2 \quad + \quad H_2O$$

$$C_4H_9OH \quad + \quad O_2 \quad \longrightarrow \quad CO_2 \quad + \quad H_2O$$

Carboxylic Acids

1. The diagram below shows the carboxylic acid methanoic acid.

a. Draw the displayed formula of the starting molecule that we use to make methanoic acid.

$+$ oxidising agent $\longrightarrow$ methanoic acid

b. Which of the following will be produced by oxidising the alcohol hexanol?

Hexene   Hexanoic acid   Hexane

---

2. The displayed formula of ethanoic acid and propanoic acid are shown below.

ethanoic acid   propanoic acid

a. Label the carboxylic acid functional group in these molecules.

b. Use the diagrams to write the structural formulas of these molecules below. The first has been done for you.

methanoic acid   ethanoic acid   propanoic acid

HCOOH

c. Explain why all of the carboxylic acids are part of the same homologous series.

d. The structural formula of butanoic acid is shown below. Draw the displayed formula of butanoic acid.

$CH_3CH_2CH_2COOH$
butanoic acid

---

3. In water, carboxylic acids ionise to release the H^+ ion. This is shown below.

$$CH_3COOH_{(aq)} \rightleftharpoons CH_3COO^-_{(aq)} + H^+_{(aq)}$$

ethanoic acid   ethanoate ion

a. Explain why carboxylic acids are weak acids.

b. Explain why carboxylic acids have a higher pH than the same concentration of a strong acid.

4. All carboxylic acids react in a similar way with metal carbonates.

a. The reaction between methanoic acid and lithium carbonate is shown below.

Complete the equation to show the products formed.

$$2\ HCOOH\ +\ Li_2CO_3\ \longrightarrow\ 2\ HCOOLi$$

methanoic acid   lithium carbonate   lithium methanoate

b. Name the products in the following reactions.

propanoic acid + sodium carbonate $\longrightarrow$

ethanoic acid + calcium carbonate $\longrightarrow$

butanoic acid + potassium carbonate $\longrightarrow$

---

5. Reacting a carboxylic acid with an alcohol makes an ester and water.

a. Why are esters useful molecules in the food industry?

The diagram below shows the reaction between ethanoic acid and ethanol.

ethanoic acid   ethanol

b. Name the ester produced in the above reaction.

c. The reaction requires sulfuric acid as a catalyst.

What is the purpose of a catalyst?

d. Forming an ester is a reversible reaction.

Using Le Chatelier's principle, describe how we can increase the yield of the ester in this reaction.

You should only refer to the concentrations of the reactants and products in this answer.

Addition Polymers

1. The diagram below shows ethene molecules joining to form poly(ethene).

a. State the name of the monomer and polymer in this reaction.

> Monomer

> Polymer

b. From the diagram, how can we tell that the polymer is an addition polymer?

c. Which of the following diagrams shows the correct repeating structure for the above polymer?

Explain why the other structures are incorrect.

$$\left(\begin{array}{c} H \ H \\ | \ \ | \\ C=C \\ | \ \ | \\ H \ H \end{array}\right)_n$$

$$\left(\begin{array}{c} H \ Br \\ | \ \ | \\ C-C \\ | \ \ | \\ H \ H \end{array}\right)_n$$

$$\left(\begin{array}{c} H \ H \\ | \ \ | \\ C-C \\ | \ \ | \\ H \ H \end{array}\right)_n$$

d. What would be the value of "n" for the polymer shown in the diagram at the top of the page?

Explain your answer.

e. Show that the atom economy of the polymerisation reaction at the top of the page is 100%.

A_r C = 12, A_r H = 1

$$\text{Atom economy} = \frac{\text{relative formula mass of desired products (from equation)}}{\text{relative formula mass of all reactants (from equation)}} \times 100$$

> **Link to Paper One**
> Atom Economy is in
> Chemistry 1
> Quantitative Chemistry

2. Draw the monomer and repeating unit for the following polymers.

a.

monomer	repeating unit

b.

$$-\underset{\underset{H}{|}}{\overset{\overset{CH_3}{|}}{C}}-\underset{\underset{H}{|}}{\overset{\overset{H}{|}}{C}}-\underset{\underset{H}{|}}{\overset{\overset{CH_3}{|}}{C}}-\underset{\underset{H}{|}}{\overset{\overset{H}{|}}{C}}-\underset{\underset{H}{|}}{\overset{\overset{CH_3}{|}}{C}}-\underset{\underset{H}{|}}{\overset{\overset{H}{|}}{C}}-\underset{\underset{H}{|}}{\overset{\overset{CH_3}{|}}{C}}-\underset{\underset{H}{|}}{\overset{\overset{H}{|}}{C}}-$$

monomer	repeating unit

3. Which of the following statements are true and which are false?

	True / False
In addition polymerisation, water is made as well as the polymer.	
In addition polymerisation, the monomers are always alkenes.	
A repeating unit always contains a double bond between the carbon atoms.	
In addition polymerisation, all of the atoms in the monomers end up in the polymer.	
Addition polymers do not have double bonds between the carbon atoms in the main chain.	

Condensation Polymers

1. The following statements apply to either addition polymers or condensation polymers.

Write "A" next to the statements for addition polymers and "C" next to the statements for condensation polymers.

Only the polymer is formed	These can be made with two monomers	The polymer and water are formed	The monomer is always an alkene

2. Two monomers used to make a condensation polymer are shown below.

```
      H  H
      |  |
H—O—C—C—O—H
      |  |
      H  H
   ethane diol
```

```
   O  H  H  H  H  O
   ||  |  |  |  |  ||
   C—C—C—C—C—C
   |  |  |  |  |  |
 H—O  H  H  H  H  O—H
       hexanedioic acid
```

a. Label the alcohol functional group on ethane diol and the carboxylic acid functional group on hexanedioic acid.

b. In the space below, draw the products formed when these two molecules react.

3. Usually, the two monomers are drawn in shorthand form.

The diagram below shows the shorthand monomers and the polymer.

HO—☐—OH   HOOC—☐—COOH

ethane diol   hexanedioic acid

HO—☐—OOC—☐—COO—☐—OOC—☐—COO—☐—OOC—☐—COOH

Polymer = poly(ester)

Draw the repeating unit for this polymer.

Amino Acids

1. The structure of the amino acid glycine is shown on the right.

a. Label the two different functional groups on the glycine molecule.

b. In the space below, draw the products formed when three glycine molecules form a polypeptide.

glycine

c. From your answer to question b, how do we know that this is a condensation polymer?

d. The shorthand form of glycine and the repeating structure of a glycine polypeptide are shown below.

glycine H_2NCH_2COOH

$\left(HNCH_2CO\right)_n$ repeating structure

Explain why the amino acid has one oxygen atom and two hydrogen atoms more than the repeating structure.

2. The diagram below shows a protein formed from glycine and another amino acid called alanine.

a. Label the functional groups in the alanine molecule.

b. How many water molecules will be produced when this protein is formed? Explain your answer.

glycine   alanine   glycine

c. Explain why the product of this reaction is a protein whereas your answer to question 1b is a polypeptide.

protein

DNA

Exam tip: You will learn much more about the structure of DNA and how it works in the Inheritance section of Biology 2.

1. Complete the sentences below by using the correct words from the list.

genetic   **develop**   **polymer**   **two**   **animals**

DNA is a _____ found in living organisms. We find DNA in _____

plants, fungi, bacteria and viruses. DNA encodes the _____ instructions that are needed

by living organisms to _____ and function. DNA consists of _____ polyme

strands wound around each other.

2. The diagram below shows two of the polymer strands in DNA.

A	T
C	G
A	T
G	C
T	A
T	A
G	C
C	G

a. What name do scientists give for the monomers in DNA?

(Nucleotides)   (Amino acids)   (Alcohols)

b. How many different monomers are used to make a DNA molecule?

c. The two polymer strands in DNA wrap around each other.

What name do scientists give to this structure?

3. Proteins, starch and cellulose are three other polymers found in living organisms.

Draw a line from the correct polymer to the correct monomer.

(Nucleotides)

(Cellulose)   (DNA)

(Glucose)

(Proteins)   (Starch)

(Amino acids)

Chapter 3: Chemical Analysis

- Describe how we can use melting and boiling point data to determine whether a substance is pure or a mixture.

- Describe what is meant by a formulation and give examples of formulations.

- Describe what is meant by the mobile phase and the stationary phase in paper chromatography.

- Explain why chemicals are separated by paper chromatography in terms of the attraction of the chemicals to the stationary phase.

- Use the results of paper chromatography to calculate the R_f value for a chemical.

- Describe how paper chromatography can be used to separate and tell the difference between coloured substances (required practical).

- Describe how to test for the gases hydrogen, oxygen, carbon dioxide and chlorine.

- Describe how to carry out a flame test to determine the presence of a metal ion.

- Describe the positive flame test results for the following metal ions: lithium, sodium, potassium, calcium and copper.

- Describe how flame emission spectroscopy can be used to analyse the metal ions present in a sample.

- Describe the advantages of instrumental techniques in analysing substances.

- Describe how sodium hydroxide can be used to identify metal ions in solution.

- State the positive sodium hydroxide tests for the following metal ions: calcium, magnesium, aluminium, copper (II), iron (II) and iron (III).

- Describe how to carry out chemical tests to identify the presence of the following non-metal ions: carbonate, halides, sulfate.

Purity and Formulations

1. The chemicals below are either pure substances or mixtures.

Above each box write "P" for pure substance or "M" for mixture.

| Sea water | Carbon dioxide | Ethane | The atmosphere | Alloys | Oxygen |

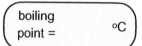

2. We can tell if a substance is pure from its melting and boiling points.

A scientist heated a sample of iodine and measured the temperature.

Their results are shown on the right.

a. Use the graph to determine the melting and boiling points of the sample of iodine.

| melting point = °C | boiling point = °C |

b. What does this tell us about the purity of the iodine?

Explain your answer.

c. Pure water has a melting point of 0°C and a boiling point of 100°C.

A scientist heated a sample of water.

Their results are shown on the left.

Explain what this shows about the purity of the sample.

3. Many mixtures are formulations.

a. What is meant by a formulation?

b. Give an example of a formulation.

Paper Chromatography

. Paper chromatography can be used to separate chemicals in a mixture.

A student wanted to work out the colours in pen ink.

The student used paper chromatography. Her results are shown on the right.

a. A solvent is a liquid which dissolves another chemical.

What is the solvent in this experiment?

b. Explain why the solvent is called the mobile phase.

c. Which part is the stationary phase?

2. Explain why the starting line is drawn in pencil.

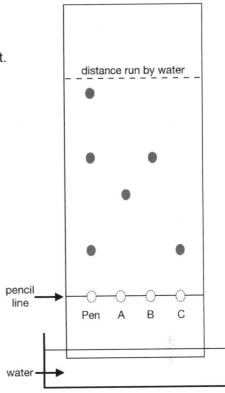

3. The experiment can be used to determine the colours in the pen ink.

a. Which colours are present in the pen ink? Explain your answer.

b. Which colour is not present in the pen ink? How do you know?

c. Why does the experiment not tell us all of the colours in the pen ink?

d. Which of the three colours (A, B or C) was least attracted to the stationary phase? Explain your answer.

4. The identity of a chemical can be determined using the Rf value.

a. Use the equation to determine the Rf value of the top colour in the pen (to 2 significant figures).

$$Rf \text{ value} = \frac{\text{distance moved by substance}}{\text{distance moved by solvent}}$$

b. Sometimes two different substances may have the same Rf value in a given solvent.

How can we overcome this problem?

Required Practical: Paper Chromatography

1. In this required practical, we will separate the food colours in a mixture.

First we draw a horizontal pencil line on the chromatography paper.

The line should be around 2 cm from the bottom of the paper.

We then make five pencil spots on the line.

Suggest why the pencil spots should not be too close together.

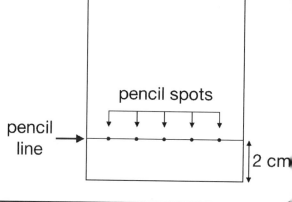

2. Using a capillary tube, we place a tiny spot of the food colouring mixture onto the first pencil spot.

We also place spots of known food colours onto the other pencil spots.

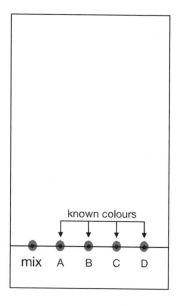

a. What is a capillary tube?

b. Why is it important that the spots of colour are very small?

3. We now pour water into a beaker to a depth of 1 cm.

Circle the correct box which describes the role of the water.

> The water is the solution

> The water is the solvent

> The water is the solute

4. We now attach the chromatography paper to a glass rod.

The paper is then lowered into the beaker and we place a lid on the beaker.

a. What is the purpose of the lid?

b. It is important that the paper does not touch the side walls of the beaker.

Suggest a reason for this.

c. Why is it important that we do not move the beaker during the experiment?

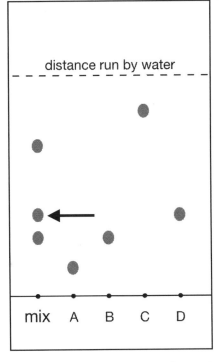

5. We stop the experiment when the water is around three quarters up the paper.

At this point, we draw a pencil line where the water reached and we leave the paper to dry.

a. What conclusions can we draw about the colours in the mix?

b. Determine the Rf value of the colour shown by the arrow (to 2 significant figures).

c. Explain why Rf values cannot always be used to identify a chemical.

Testing for Gases

1. Imagine that we have a test tube that may contain hydrogen gas.

To test for hydrogen, we remove the bung and rapidly insert a lit splint.

a. What will we hear if hydrogen gas is present?

The equation for the reaction between hydrogen and oxygen (in the air) is shown below.

$$\underline{\hspace{1cm}} H_{2\,(g)} \quad + \quad O_{2\,(g)} \quad \longrightarrow \quad \underline{\hspace{1cm}} H_2O_{(l)}$$

b. Balance the equation by writing large numbers in the spaces shown.

c. What is meant by the small letters "g" and "l" in the equation?

---

2. To test for oxygen gas, we insert a glowing splint into the test tube.

What will we see if oxygen gas is present?

| The splint will change colour | The splint will go out | The splint will relight |

---

3. To test for carbon dioxide, we bubble the gas through limewater.

Limewater is an aqueous solution of calcium hydroxide.

The formula of calcium hydroxide is shown on the right.

$$Ca(OH)_{2\,(\ldots\ldots)}$$

a. Complete the formula to show the state symbol for an aqueous solution.

b. What will we see if the gas is carbon dioxide?

---

4. To test for chlorine gas, we place damp litmus paper near the mouth of the test tube.

What will we see if the test tube contains chlorine gas?

---

5. The gas tests are summarised below. Write the name of the gas above each test.

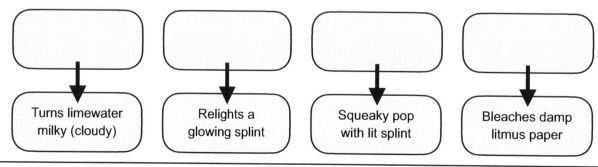

| Turns limewater milky (cloudy) | Relights a glowing splint | Squeaky pop with lit splint | Bleaches damp litmus paper |

Flame Tests

1. Flame tests can be used to identify metal ions.

a. Describe how to carry out a flame test.

b. Draw lines to link the correct metal ion to the correct colour.

Calcium ion	Orange - Red
Copper ion	Crimson
Lithium ion	Green
Sodium ion	Lilac
Potassium ion	Yellow

c. State the colour produced by the following compounds when placed in a blue Bunsen burner flame.

$LiNO_3$ colour =	CaF_2 colour =	$CuCl_2$ colour =	K_2O colour =	Na_2SO_4 colour =

d. Complete the sentences below by using the correct words from the list.

concentration　　　　**mixture**　　　　**rapid**　　　　**colour**　　　　**sensitivity**

Flame tests are a _____ and easy way to identify metal ions. However, there are two

problems with flame tests. Firstly, they have a low _____ . In other words it can be very

difficult to determine the _____ of the flame by eye. This is especially the case when

the metal ion is present in a very low_____ . Secondly, flame tests cannot be used

to determine the metal ions present in a _____ .

2. Another way to identify metal ions is to use Flame emission spectroscopy.

In Flame emission spectroscopy, the metal ion in solution is placed into a flame.

The light from the flame is then passed through a spectroscope which splits the light into a spectrum.

The diagrams below show the spectra produced from different metal ions.

Metal Ion A

Metal Ion B

Metal Ion C

a. A scientist analysed a mixture of different samples of metal ions.

This is shown below.

Describe what the spectrum shows and explain your answer.

b. The scientist analysed another sample which was NOT a mixture.

This is shown below.

Describe what this spectrum shows.

Flame emission spectroscopy is an example of an instrumental technique.

c. Describe three advantages of using instrumental techniques to analyse substances.

Metal Hydroxide Precipitates

1. Certain metal ions form a precipitate with sodium hydroxide solution.

a. Describe what we see if we add sodium hydroxide solution to the following metal ions.

calcium ion ⟶

magnesium ion ⟶

aluminium ion ⟶ excess sodium hydroxide solution ⟶

b. Two of the reactions with sodium hydroxide solution are shown below.

Balance the equations and insert the correct state symbols in the spaces.

| sodium hydroxide solution | + | calcium chloride solution | ⟶ | calcium hydroxide precipitate | + | sodium chloride solution |

| _____ NaOH (aq) | + | CaCl$_2$ (aq) | ⟶ | Ca(OH)$_2$ ( ) | + | 2 NaCl (aq) |

| sodium hydroxide solution | + | aluminium nitrate solution | ⟶ | aluminium hydroxide precipitate | + | sodium nitrate solution |

| _____ NaOH (aq) | + | Al(NO$_3$)$_3$ (aq) | ⟶ | Al(OH)$_3$ ( ) | + | _____ NaNO$_3$ (aq) |

c. Sodium hydroxide solution also forms precipitates with other metal ions.

Complete the boxes below to show the colours of the precipitates formed.

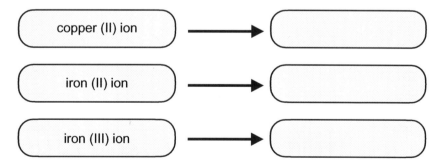

copper (II) ion ⟶

iron (II) ion ⟶

iron (III) ion ⟶

d. Complete the equation for the reaction below.

| sodium hydroxide solution | + | iron (II) bromide solution | ⟶ | iron hydroxide precipitate | + | sodium chloride solution |

| _____ NaOH (aq) | + | FeBr$_2$ (aq) | ⟶ | _____ ( ) | + | 2 NaCl (aq) |

Identifying Non-Metal Ions

1. The carbonate ion is found in chemicals such as sodium carbonate Na_2CO_3.

Metal carbonates produce carbon dioxide gas when reacted with acid. This is the basis for the carbonate test.

a. Complete the boxes below to show the stages of the test for the carbonate ion.

| stage 1 | stage 2 | stage 3 | stage 4 |

Add any dilute _____ to the sample

If you see _____ collect the gas

Bubble the gas through _____

If limewater turns milky then the gas is _____

➡ **Positive test for carbonate ion**

b. Explain why we can use any acid in this test.

c. Explain why effervescence is not enough to prove the presence of the carbonate ion.

---

2. The test for halide ions is shown on the right.

a. Complete the boxes to show the stages.

b. In the first stage of the halide test, we add nitric acid.

Suggest why we cannot use hydrochloric acid.

c. Suggest the name of the compound formed with a positive test for the chloride ion.

Add _____ to the sample

⬇

Add _____ solution

⬇

| Chloride ion = | Bromide ion = | Iodide ion = |

Chloride ion = _____ precipitate

Bromide ion = _____ precipitate

Iodide ion = _____ precipitate

---

3. The test for the sulfate ion is shown below.

a. Complete the boxes to show the stages.

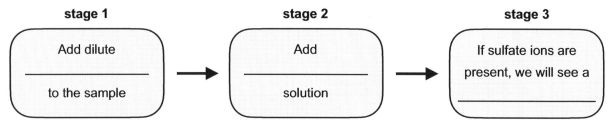

| stage 1 | stage 2 | stage 3 |

Add dilute _____ to the sample

➡ Add _____ solution

➡ If sulfate ions are present, we will see a _____

b. Explain why we could not use sulfuric acid in stage 1.

Required Practical: Identifying Ions

1. A scientist has a sample which may contain potassium carbonate.

Describe how the scientist could check the following:

a. That the compound contains the potassium ion.

b. That the compound contains the carbonate ion.

2. A scientist has a sample which may contain magnesium chloride.

Describe how the scientist could check the following:

a. That the compound contains the magnesium ion.

b. That the compound contains the chloride ion.

3. A scientist has a sample which may contain copper (II) sulfate.

Describe how the scientist could check the following:

a. That the compound contains the copper (II) ion.

b. That the compound contains the sulfate ion.

4. Describe how a scientist could confirm that a compound is aluminium iodide.

5. A scientist carried out the following tests on a compound.

- A flame test produced a yellow flame.
- When treated with dilute nitric acid followed by silver nitrate solution, a cream precipitate was produced.

Identify the compound.

6. A scientist carried out the following tests on a compound.

- Reacting with dilute sodium hydroxide solution produced a brown precipitate.
- When treated with hydrochloric acid followed by barium chloride solution, a white precipitate was produced.

Identify the compound.

7. A scientist carried out the following tests on a compound.

- A flame test produced a crimson flame.
- When treated with dilute nitric acid followed by silver nitrate solution, a yellow precipitate was produced.

Identify the compound.

8. Describe how a scientist could confirm that a compound is calcium carbonate.

Chapter 4: The Atmosphere

- State the gases present in the atmosphere today and the proportions of oxygen and nitrogen in the atmosphere.

- State the gases that scientists think were present in the early atmosphere.

- State the planets which have an atmosphere today which is similar to the early atmosphere of the Earth.

- Describe the changes which have taken place as the atmosphere developed from its early stages to its composition today.

- Describe the role of photosynthesis in the changes that took place in the atmosphere.

- Describe examples of fossil fuels and explain how coal, oil and natural gas are formed.

- Explain why fossil fuels are non-renewable.

- State examples of greenhouse gases.

- Describe in terms of short and long wavelength radiation how greenhouse gases affect the temperature of the atmosphere.

- Describe how combustion of fossil fuels, deforestation and agriculture are leading to climate change.

- Describe the possible effects of climate change.

- Explain what is meant by peer review.

- Explain why media reports about climate change may not alway be accurate.

- Describe what is meant by the carbon footprint.

- Describe what humans can do to reduce their carbon footprint.

- Describe the pollutants that can be produced by combusting fossil fuels and the effects of these pollutants.

The Atmosphere

1. The diagram below shows the gases in the atmosphere today.

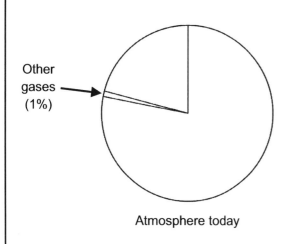

Other gases (1%)

Atmosphere today

a. Label the diagram to show the two most common gases in the current atmosphere.

Show the approximate percentage of each gas.

b. One of the "other gases" in the atmosphere is argon.

Argon is a noble gas.

In which group of the periodic table do we find the noble gases?

Link to Paper One
Group 0 is in Chemistry 1 Atomic Structure and the Periodic Table

Group 1   Group 7   Group 0

c. Apart from argon, give examples of two of the "other gases" in the atmosphere today.

---

2. The atmosphere has underwent major changes in the history of the Earth.

a. Why can scientists not be certain about the gases in the early atmosphere?

b. The diagram shows the gases that scientists think formed the early atmosphere.

Describe three differences in the gases between the early atmosphere and the atmosphere today.

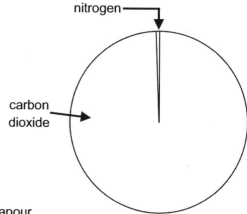

nitrogen

carbon dioxide

c. Volcanoes released a large amount of carbon dioxide and water vapour.

Give three examples of other gases released by volcanoes.

d. Describe how the Earth's early atmosphere was very similar to the atmospheres of Mars and Venus today.

3. Over many millions of years, the level of carbon dioxide in the early atmosphere began to fall.

Complete the boxes below to show how the level of carbon dioxide decreased.

Early Earth

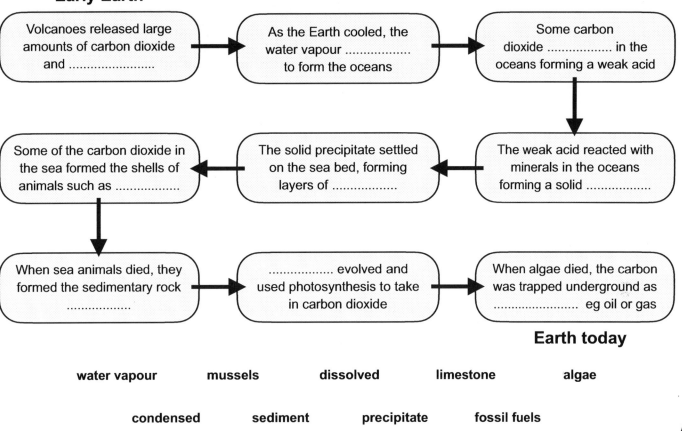

Volcanoes released large amounts of carbon dioxide and ....

As the Earth cooled, the water vapour .... to form the oceans

Some carbon dioxide .... in the oceans forming a weak acid

Some of the carbon dioxide in the sea formed the shells of animals such as ....

The solid precipitate settled on the sea bed, forming layers of ....

The weak acid reacted with minerals in the oceans forming a solid ....

When sea animals died, they formed the sedimentary rock ....

.... evolved and used photosynthesis to take in carbon dioxide

When algae died, the carbon was trapped underground as .... eg oil or gas

Earth today

water vapour   **mussels**   **dissolved**   **limestone**   **algae**

condensed   **sediment**   **precipitate**   **fossil fuels**

4. One of the most important stages was the evolution of algae which can carry out photosynthesis.

a. When do scientists think that algae first evolved?

2.7 million years ago

270 million years ago

2.7 billion years ago

b. The equation for photosynthesis is shown below.

Balance the equation by inserting large numbers into the spaces.

$$\text{carbon dioxide} \quad + \quad \text{water} \quad \xrightarrow{\text{light}} \quad \text{glucose} \quad + \quad \text{oxygen}$$

$$\_\_\_\_ CO_2 \qquad\qquad \_\_\_\_ H_2O \qquad\qquad C_6H_{12}O_6 \qquad 6\,O_2$$

c. Explain how the evolution of algae and photosynthetic plants allowed the evolution of animals.

Fossil Fuels

1. Fossil fuels form over millions of years. You need to be able to describe how these are formed.

a. All fossil fuels contain the element carbon. How is this carbon first taken in to form fossil fuels?

| The carbon is part of the carbon dioxide released during combustion | The carbon is part of the carbon dioxide taken in by plants during photosynthesis | The carbon is part of the carbon dioxide released by plants during respiration |

b. Fossil fuels are non-renewable. What does this mean?

---

2. The formation of coal is shown below.

| Coal is formed from the remains of trees and ferns | → | In marshy wetlands the plant remains do not decompose | → | Over time, a layer of sediment compresses the plant remains | → | | → **COAL** |

a. Tick the boxes which show the conditions in marshy wetlands.

| Acidic | Lots of oxygen | Neutral | No oxygen |

b. Explain how these conditions prevent the plant remains from decomposing.

c. Complete the box to show the final conditions that convert the plant remains into coal.

---

3. The formation of oil is shown below.

| Oil forms from the remains of tiny sea creatures called plankton which settle in mud on the sea bed | → | If oxygen is not present, the plankton remains do not decompose | → | The remains are compressed by a layer of sediment at high temperature and pressure | → **OIL** |

a. How is the starting material for oil different from the starting material for coal?

b. Why do the plankton remains not decompose in the mud on the sea bed?

---

4. Natural gas is mainly the hydrocarbon methane.

Explain why natural gas is often found near oil deposits.

The Greenhouse Effect

1. The Earth's atmosphere contains three major greenhouse gases.

a. State the names of these gases and write the amount of each gas in the Earth's atmosphere.

b. The diagram below shows the greenhouse effect in terms of radiation.

Complete the diagram using the information below.

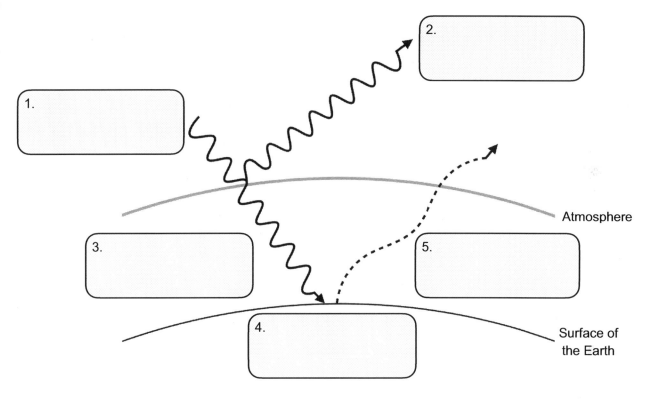

The surface of the Earth absorbs the energy and radiates long wavelength radiation	Most of the short wavelength radiation passes through the atmosphere	Greenhouse gases absorb some of the energy of the long wavelength radiation	Some of the short wavelength radiation reflects back into space	Energy from the Sun travels to the Earth as short wavelength radiation

c. Three types of radiation are shown below. Which are long wavelength (L) and which are short wavelength (S)?

ultraviolet =   infrared =   visible light =

d. Why does the greenhouse effect increase the temperature of the atmosphere?

e. Explain why the greenhouse effect has been essential for the development of life on Earth.

Climate Change

1. Both carbon dioxide and methane are greenhouse gases and their levels in the atmosphere are increasing.

a. Describe how fossil fuel use and deforestation are leading to climate change.

Fossil fuels	Deforestation
•	• ....

b. How is agriculture causing the level of methane in the atmosphere to increase?

c. Describe how each of the following could be affected by climate change.

Global ice and sea levels	Weather	Insects

2. A large number of scientists currently work on climate change.

Complete the sentences below by using the correct words from the list.

valid   simplified   evidence   atmosphere   greenhouse   peer   bias   speculation   complex

Many scientists believe that climate change is caused by the release of _____ gases by

human activities. Scientists share their _____ with other scientists who can criticise the

data and decide whether it is _____ . This process is called _____ review.

This can be used to detect data which may show _____ . One of the problems with

climate change is that it is _____ and difficult to model. This means that media reports

about climate change can be biased or over-_____ . Another problem is that scientists

cannot be certain about how much the temperature of the _____ will increase.

This has led to wild _____ in the media. Scientists must work harder to educate the

public about the issues around climate change.

Carbon Footprint

1. Many people are keen to reduce their carbon footprint.

a. Complete the sentences below by selecting the correct words from the boxes.

The carbon footprint is the total amount of
| oxygen |
| argon |
| carbon dioxide |
and other greenhouse gases emitted over the full

| disposal |
| lifecycle |
| manufacture |
of a product, service or event. We can use this to find ways to reduce
| climate change |
| waste |
| pollution |
.

b. All of the changes below can reduce our carbon footprint.

For each change, draw a line to show which gas it reduces and then describe how it has this effect.

| Install more effective home insulation |

| Encourage the use of public transport |

| Carbon dioxide |

| Methane |

| Use renewable sources of electricity |

| Eat less beef and dairy products |

c. Apart from using renewable sources, how else can we reduce our carbon footprint due to electricity use?

d. Landfills can release methane. This can be trapped and burned to generate electricity.

Describe why this is better than releasing the methane into the atmosphere.

e. Describe two reasons why people may not be willing to reduce their carbon footprint.

Pollutants from Fuels

1. When we burn fuels such as coal and petrol we release energy.

a. Hydrocarbons such as petrol are used to power vehicles. Coal is used to generate electricity.

The equation below shows the combustion of methane. Balance the equation by writing a large number in the space.

methane	+	oxygen	$\longrightarrow$	carbon dioxide	+	water
CH_4		____ O_2		CO_2		$2\,H_2O$

b. In this reaction, the carbon and hydrogen atoms have been oxidised. What does this mean?

c. How can we tell from the equation that this is complete combustion?

Water has been produced in the reaction	Oxygen has been used in the reaction	Carbon dioxide has been produced in the reaction

d. If the amount of oxygen is reduced, then incomplete combustion takes place.

Incomplete combustion produces carbon monoxide. Explain why this is dangerous.

---

2. Two other pollutants are sulfur dioxide and oxides of nitrogen.

a. Describe how these two pollutants are formed.

Sulfur dioxide	Oxides of nitrogen

b. When these gases dissolve in rainwater, they form acid rain.

State two harmful effects of acid rain.

---

3. Burning fossil fuels can release particulates such as carbon particles. These are linked to global dimming.

a. Describe what is meant by global dimming.

b. What is the effect of carbon particles on human health?

Chapter 5: Resources

- Describe how humans use the Earth's resources.

- Describe what is meant by finite and renewable resources.

- Describe what is meant by potable water and explain how this is produced from fresh water and salt water.

- Describe how to analyse water from different sources and how to purify water using distillation (required practical).

- Describe the stages in purifying waste water from domestic, agricultural and industrial uses.

- Explain why we need to extract metals from low-grade sources.

- Describe how metals can be extracted by phytomining and bioleaching.

- Describe the stages of a life-cycle assessment.

- Carry out a life-cycle assessment for plastic shopping bags and paper shopping bags.

- Explain why it is important that materials are reused or recycled.

- Describe what is meant by corrosion and rusting.

- Describe the different factors that are required for metals to corrode.

- Explain how corrosion can be prevented by coating and by galvanising.

- Describe what is meant by an alloy and explain why alloys are harder than pure metals.

- Describe what is meant by ceramics and by composites.

- Describe the properties of thermosoftening and thermosetting polymers and explain how their structures lead to these properties.

- Describe how ammonia can be produced by the Haber Process.

- Describe the role of NPK fertilisers and explain how these are produced.

Using the Earth's Resources

1. Humans use the Earth's resources for a range of different reasons.

Complete the sentences below by using the correct words from the list.

| offices | crops | transport | fossil fuels | concrete | cars | food | warmth |

Humans use resources to provide _____ for example burning wood or _____ .

Resources are also used to grow _____ or raise animals for _____ . Homes,

factories and _____ are built from wood, _____ , glass and bricks. These

provide us with shelter. Lastly, many different resources are used to build and to power _____ ,

airplanes and trains. These provide us with _____ .

2. Many resources are provided by farming and agriculture.

a. Describe how farmed resources are used to provide the following:

| materials for clothing | fuels |

b. Rubber comes from the sap of rubber trees which are grown in large plantations.

Describe how Chemistry has provided an alternative to farmed rubber.

c. Describe the difference between finite resources and renewable resources.

d. The following natural resources are either finite or renewable.

Write "F" above the finite resources and "R" above the renewable resources.

| aluminium | fish | wood | olive oil | crude oil | cocoa beans | coal |

e. Human activity should be sustainable. Explain what is meant by this in the space below.

Potable Water

1. Drinking water is essential for human life.

Decide whether each of the following statements are true or false. Write the correct versions of the false statements.

| Drinking water can have low levels of dissolved salts eg sodium chloride | True / False ⟶ |

| Drinking water can contain quite high levels of microbes eg bacteria | True / False ⟶ |

| Potable water is water that is safe to drink | True / False ⟶ |

| Pure water can have low levels of dissolved substances | True / False ⟶ |

| Potable water is the same as pure water | True / False ⟶ |

2. In the UK, most of our potable water comes from rain water.

a. What is the main advantage of rain water as a source of potable water?

b. Rainwater is also called "fresh water".

Which of the following are sources of fresh water in the UK? Tick the correct boxes.

| Rivers | Lakes | Seawater |
| Underground sources (aquifers) | Reservoirs (man-made lakes) | Treated sewage |

3. The stages for producing potable water are shown below.

a. Complete the flowchart and answer the questions next to each stage.

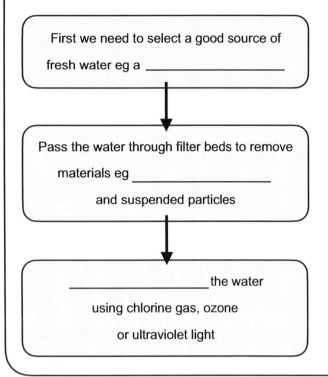

First we need to select a good source of

fresh water eg a _____

Pass the water through filter beds to remove

materials eg _____

and suspended particles

_____ the water

using chlorine gas, ozone

or ultraviolet light

b. Suggest why we would not take fresh water from a river running too close to a farm.

c. Why do you think that filter beds cannot remove microbes such as bacteria?

d. What is the purpose of this stage?

---

4. Remember that fresh water can have low levels of dissolved minerals.

In some parts of the world, fresh water is very limited. They get their potable water from seawater.

a. Explain why humans cannot drink untreated seawater.

b. Before drinking, seawater undergoes desalination. What is the purpose of desalination?

> **Link to Paper One**
> Distillation is found in
> Chemistry 1 Atomic Structure
> and the Periodic Table

c. Desalination can be carried out by reverse osmosis or distillation.

Describe what happens in these two processes.

Reverse osmosis	Distillation

d. What is the disadvantage of these two methods of desalination?

Required Practical: Water

1. This required practical consists of two parts.

In the first part, we will check to see whether a sample of water is pure.

a. State two differences between pure water and potable water.

pipette

water sample

b. First we need to check the pH of the water sample.

To do this, we add a drop of the water to a piece of universal indicator paper.

State the pH shown by the following colours of universal indicator:

universal indicator paper

Red = pH _____   Green = pH _____   Purple = pH _____

c. Explain why a pH of 7 does not tell us that the water sample is pure.

2. We now need to check that the water sample does not contain any dissolved solids.

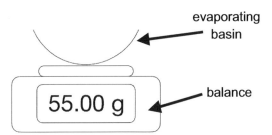

evaporating basin

balance

a. First we use a balance to find the mass of an empty evaporating basin.

Which of the following is the resolution of the balance shown?

| 1 g | 0.1 g | 0.01 g |

b. We now fill the evaporating basin with water and heat gently with a Bunsen burner until there is no water left.

Explain what is happening to the water during this stage.

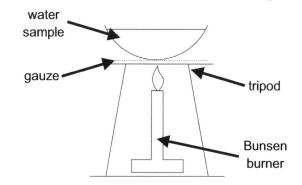

water sample

gauze

tripod

Bunsen burner

c. We now allow the evaporating basin to cool and find the new mass.

How will the results tell us if the water sample was pure?

Explain your answer.

3. The table below shows the results of the experiment for three samples of water, all with a pH of 7.

	Water sample A	Water sample B	Water sample C
Mass of evaporating basin at start in grams	54.74	53.22	56.87
Mass of evaporating basin at end in grams	55.55	53.22	56.65

a. Which water sample was pure?   Pure water =

b. One of the results is anomalous. Identify the anomalous result.   Anomalous result =

c. Which of the following could explain the anomalous result?

The evaporating basin was heated for too long

The evaporating basin contained some water when it was first weighed

The evaporating basin was not heated for long enough

---

4. In the second part of this required practical, we purify water by using distillation.

a. The apparatus is shown below. Label the diagram using the labels on the right.

delivery tube

iced water

pure water

water sample

conical flask

test tube

b. Label the part of the diagram where the water evaporates to form water vapour.

c. Label the part of the diagram where the water vapour condenses to form liquid water.

d. Explain why iced water is used in the beaker.

e. Explain why distillation is an expensive way to purify water.

Waste Water Treatment

1. Human activity uses a great deal of water.

a. Some of this is used in homes, some in agriculture and some in industry (eg factories).

Above each box, write "H" if the water is used in homes, "A" if it is used in agriculture and "I" if it is used in industry.

Manufacturing clothes	Drinking water for cattle	Watering crops	Manufacturing paper	Bathing and showering

Preparing food	Drinking	Flushing the toilet	Manufacturing chemicals	Manufacturing computers

b. Give two reasons why waste water from homes and farms cannot be returned directly back to rivers.

2. The stages in waste water treatment are shown below.

Screening

↓

Sedimentation

Effluent   Sludge

↓   ↓

Aerobic digestion   Anaerobic digestion

↓   ↓

Returned to waterways   Fertiliser for farming

a. What is the purpose of screening?

b. Describe what happens during sedimentation.

c. The sludge undergoes anaerobic digestion. What happens during this process?

d. Anaerobic digestion produces biogas. How is this used?

e. Suggest why sludge makes such a useful fertiliser.

3. The effluent undergoes aerobic digestion before being returned to waterways such as rivers.

Complete the sentences below by using the correct words from the list.

aerobic   aquatic   oxygen   reduced   microorganisms   organic   liquid

Effluent is the _____ part of sewage formed during sedimentation. Effluent contains a

very large amount of _____ molecules and harmful _____. If we

simply returned the effluent to waterways, it would kill _____ organisms such as fish.

To prevent this, the effluent undergoes digestion by _____ bacteria. Air is bubbled

through the effluent to provide _____ . After aerobic digestion, levels of organic molecules

and harmful microorganisms are_____ to safe levels. Now the effluent can be safely

discharged into waterways or the sea.

---

4. A lot of waste water is produced from factories and other industries.

This water contains a large number of harmful chemicals.

Suggest two reasons why the chemicals must be removed before the waste water can enter the sewage system.

---

5. Potable water can be made from ground water (such as aquifers), waste water and sea water.

Each source has advantages and disadvantages.

a. Describe how ground water from aquifers is treated before it is potable water.

b. Explain why making potable water from waste water is only carried out where water is scarce.

c. Producing potable water from sea water is expensive.

Explain why.

Alternative Methods of Extracting Metals

1. Humans use millions of tons of metal every year.

One of the most important is copper.

a. Which of the following is the main use of copper?

| Manufacturing plastics eg for furniture and packaging | Producing electronic equipment such as phones and computers | Producing ceramic materials eg cups and plates |

b. Complete the sentences below by selecting the correct words from the boxes.

Metals such as copper are extracted from ores. These contain enough metal to make it

> easy
> economical
> rapid

to extract the metal. Copper ores are becoming

> polluted
> contaminated
> scarce

in other words they are running out. This

means that we now have to use

> low grade
> abundant
> rich

ores which contain only a small amount of copper. It is

harder to extract copper economically from low grade ores. One way is to use phytomining.

2. The stages in phytomining are shown below.

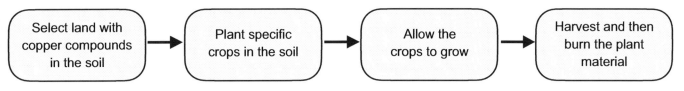

Select land with copper compounds in the soil → Plant specific crops in the soil → Allow the crops to grow → Harvest and then burn the plant material

a. As the plants grow, what do they do to the metal compounds in the soil?

b. When the plants are burned, what can we say about the level of copper compound in the ash?

3. Another way to extract metal from low grade ore is to use bioleaching.

The stages in bioleaching are shown below.

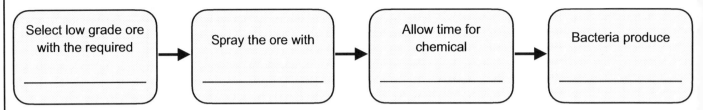

| Select low grade ore with the required _____ | → | Spray the ore with _____ | → | Allow time for chemical _____ | → | Bacteria produce _____ |

a. Complete each stage by selecting the correct words from the list below.

reactions   **metal compound**   **leachate**   **bacteria**

b. What can we say about the level of metal compound in the leachate compared to the ore?

---

4. After both phytomining and bioleaching, we have to extract the copper from the copper compound.

One way of doing this is to displace the copper using iron.

a. What does this tell us about the reactivity of iron compared to copper?

Explain your answer.

b. State another process that can be used to extract the copper from the copper compound.

---

5. Both phytomining and bioleaching allow us to economically extract metal from low grade ores.

a. Explain why the amount of high grade ore remaining in the Earth makes this important.

b. Describe an advantage of phytomining and bioleaching compared to traditional mining.

Life Cycle Assessment

1. The first part of a life cycle assessment looks at the raw materials used to make a product.

a. Many products contain plastics (polymers). The stages in producing plastics are shown below.

Hydrocarbons separated	Manufacture of the polymer	Transport of oil to refineries	Crude oil extracted from the ground	Cracking to produce alkenes

Write the stages in the correct order in the boxes below.

Stage 1	Stage 2	Stage 3	Stage 4	Stage 5

b. Each stage in producing plastics can contribute to climate change. Explain why.

c. Many products contain metals. Explain why producing metals is harmful to the environment.

Mining and transport of metal ore	Extraction of the metal from the ore

2. The next two parts of a life cycle assessment look at how the product is manufactured and then used.

a. Which of the following show ways that manufacturing a product can harm the environment?

Circle the correct boxes.

Production of waste when raw materials are extracted	Release of harmful chemicals from factories	Disposal of the product in landfills	Energy required by machines in factories

b. Explain how toys can cause damage to the environment when they are used.

3. Finally, we need to consider how a product is disposed of at the end of its life.

Describe two ways that disposing of a product requires energy.

4. In the exam, you could be asked to compare the effects of plastic bags and paper bags on the environment.

a. Complete the table below looking at different effects of these two types of bags.

	Plastic bags	Paper bags
Extraction of raw materials	Plastic bags are produced using crude oil. Crude oil is a non-renewable resource. It could eventually run out.	
		Cutting down trees in forests can destroy habitats for animals and plants.
Manufacturing	Manufacturing plastics needs a lot of energy. If this is generated by burning fossil fuels then this contributes to climate change. Harmful waste chemicals are also produced.	
Lifetime use		Paper bags are not strong and are generally only used once before being thrown away.
Disposal	Plastic bags are not heavy so transportation to landfill does not require a lot of energy. Plastic bags are non-biodegradable (they are not broken down by microorganisms). They last for many years in the environment and fill up landfills.	

b. Life cycle assessments are not a perfect way to work out the effect of products on the environment.

Describe two problems with life cycle assessments.

Recycling

1. Humans use a great deal of different materials eg glass, plastic and metals.

It is extremely important that we try to recycle materials rather than make new ones from raw materials.

a. Complete the boxes below to show why it is important that we try to recycle materials.

Availability of raw materials	Extraction of raw materials	Manufacture of finished product

b. Explain why recycling is important in terms of waste.

2. Glass and plastic are two materials that we use a lot for example glass jars and plastic bottles.

Describe how we can reuse or recycle glass and plastic objects.

3. Some metals are now becoming scarce so it is very important that we recycle them.

The stages in recycling metals are shown on the left.

a. Explain why separating the scrap metals can increase the cost of recycling metals.

Collect scrap metal eg cars

↓

Separate different metals

↓

b. Steel is an alloy containing iron with other metals.

To recycle steel we can add it to iron in a blast furnace.

Describe two reasons why this is better than producing fresh iron from iron ore.

Link to Paper One
Alloys are found in Chemistry 1 Structure and Bonding

Melt metal

↓

Recast metal into new product

Corrosion

1. Corrosion can be a major problem for many different materials.

a. Complete the sentences below by using the correct words from the list.

| **corrosion** | **iron** | **steel** | **destruction** | **rusting** | **reactions** |

Corrosion is the _____ of materials by chemical _____ with substances

in the environment. A good example of corrosion is _____ . This only ever applies to

materials containing _____ or alloys of iron such as _____ . For metals

other than iron or alloys of iron, we should say _____ not rusting.

b. We have already seen corrosion in the topic on the atmosphere.

Which type of building material is corroded by acid rain?

Glass   Aluminium   Limestone

2. The following experiment can be used to test the conditions required for rusting.

The test tubes below are set up and left for several days.

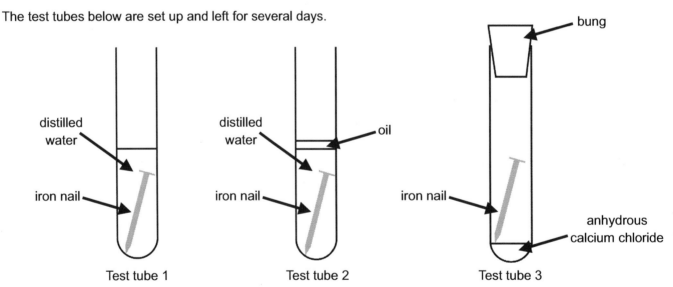

Test tube 1   Test tube 2   Test tube 3

a. The distilled water has been boiled before being placed in the test tubes. Explain the purpose of this.

b. Why is oil placed on the water in test tube number 2?

c. What is the purpose of the anhydrous calcium chloride in test tube number 3?

d. Explain why a bung has been fitted to test tube number 3.

e. What will we see after several days?

Rusting in test tubes 1 and 2 only	Rusting in test tube 1 only	Rusting in test tube 2 only	Rusting in all three test tubes

f. What does the experiment tell us about the conditions required for rusting?

---

3. We can prevent corrosion by covering the object with paint or grease or by electroplating.

a. Explain how these three methods prevent corrosion.

b. Why does aluminium not require any protection from corrosion?

---

4. Another way of preventing corrosion is to galvanise the object.

a. What is meant by galvanising?

b. Galvanising protects the object by coating it.

How else does galvanising protect iron objects from corrosion?

c. What do scientists call this type of protection?

Reactive protection	Sacrificial protection	Corrosion protection

Alloys

1. Alloys are often more useful than the pure form of metals.

a. Describe how an alloy is made.

b. The diagram below shows the arrangement of atoms in a pure metal and an alloy.

Pure metal   Alloy

Use the arrangement of atoms to explain why alloys are harder than pure metals.

2. Bronze and brass are two alloys of the metal copper.

The two alloys have different properties and are used for different purposes.

Complete the boxes about bronze and brass using the information below.

This is an alloy of copper and zinc	**This alloy is used to make door handles**
This alloy does not corrode	**This alloy is soft enough to shape**

This alloy is used to make statues	**This alloy is extremely hard**
This is an alloy of copper and tin	**This alloy is used to make musical instruments**

3. Gold is another metal which is usually made into an alloy.

Complete the sentences below by selecting the correct words from the boxes.

Gold is used to make jewellery but pure gold is too

| expensive |
| hard |
| soft |

. To make gold alloys, pure gold is mixed

with

| aluminium |
| silver |
| lead |

copper and zinc. The purity of gold is rated in carats. Gold which is 100% pure has a

carat rating of 24 whereas 18 carat gold only contains

| 75% |
| 50% |
| 25% |

gold.

---

4. Steel is an alloy of iron. There are lots of different kinds of steel.

a. Draw lines to link the type of steel to its property and then its use.

| High carbon steel | This steel is soft enough to easily shape | This steel is used to make car bodies |

| Low carbon steel | Contains chromium and nickel which prevent rusting | This steel is used to make tools eg chisels |

| Stainless steel | This steel is extremely hard but also brittle | This steel is used to make knives and forks |

b. Explain why high carbon steel is harder than low carbon steel.

You will need to discuss the arrangement of atoms in your answer.

---

5. Alloys of aluminium are used to make airplane bodies.

Describe the property of these alloys which make them useful for this purpose.

Ceramics and Composites

1. Glass is an example of a ceramic.

There are two different types of glass.

a. Complete the flow chart to show how how these types of glass are made.

b. What items are made from soda-lime glass?

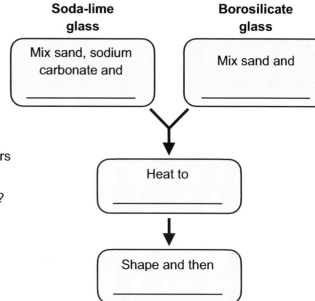

c. Borosilicate glass is used to make labware such as beakers as well as kitchenware such as casserole dishes.

What property of borosilicate glass makes it useful for these?

d. How are clay ceramics different to glass, in terms of their raw material and how they are made?

---

2. Composites are made by combining two materials:

The reinforcement gives the composite strength and the matrix (or binder) gives the composite structure.

a. Carbon fibre composite is used to make cars and aircraft parts.

State the reinforcement and matrix in carbon fibre composite.

Reinforcement =

Matrix =

b. Why is carbon fibre composite useful for making cars and aircraft parts?

c. Reinforced concrete is another composite material.

State the reinforcement and matrix in reinforced concrete.

Reinforcement =

Matrix =

d. Why is reinforced concrete useful for making buildings?

Thermosoftening and Thermosetting Polymers

Exam tip: This topic looks at how the bonding in a material affects its properties. This overlaps with Paper 1 Structure and Bonding which is one of the topics that can be revisited in Paper 2.

1. Polymers have a range of different uses, depending on their properties.

a. What do we call the small molecules that polymers are made from?

> Alkanes   Hydrocarbons   Monomers

b. Polymers can have a range of properties. These include hardness and density.

State three conditions used in manufacturing the polymer that can affect the polymer's properties.

2. Thermosoftening polymers melt when heated.

We can then reshape them and cool them back to a solid.

This is shown in the diagram on the right.

a. Label the diagram to show:

- The polymer strands

- The intermolecular forces of attraction

b. Explain why thermosoftening polymers can melt when heated and reform when cooled.

Heat

Cool

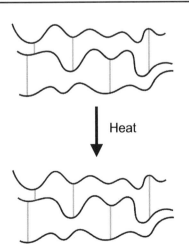

Heat

3. Thermosetting polymers do not melt when heated.

The structure of a thermosetting polymer is shown on the left.

a. Label the diagram to show the bonding in a thermosetting polymer.

b. Explain why thermosetting polymers do not melt when heated.

The Haber Process

1. The Haber process is used to make ammonia.

The equation for the Haber process is shown below.

$$N_2 \; (\ldots\ldots) \quad + \quad \underline{}H_2 \; (\ldots\ldots) \quad \rightleftharpoons \quad \underline{}NH_3 \; (\ldots\ldots)$$

a. Balance the equation and write the state symbols in the spaces.

b. State a use for the ammonia produced by the Haber process.

c. A scientist reacted 56 g of nitrogen with excess hydrogen. 17 g of ammonia was produced.

Calculate the percentage yield for this reaction. A_r N = 14, A_r H = 1

> **Link to Paper One**
> Percentage Yield is found
> in Chemistry 1
> Quantitative Chemistry

d. Explain why the yield of the Haber process will not be 100%.

2. The stages in the production of ammonia are shown below.

a. Describe how we obtain the starting materials for the Haber process.

b. Explain why the unreacted nitrogen and hydrogen are recirculated back over the catalyst.

c. Explain how removing the ammonia produced in the reaction increases the yield.

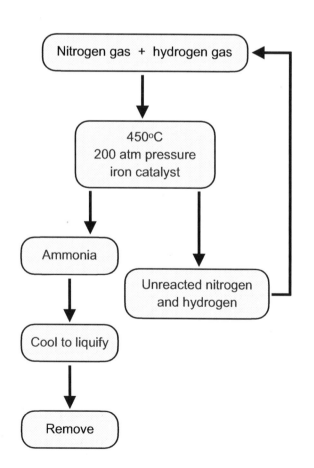

3. We can adjust the conditions of the Haber process to push the equilibrium towards the products.

To do this, we need to use Le Chatelier's principle.

a. State Le Chatelier's principle.

The Haber process is an exothermic reaction.

b. Draw the energy profile for an exothermic reaction in the space below.

c. Ideally, the Haber process should be carried out at a relatively cool temperature.

Explain why.

The graph shows the effect of changing conditions on the Haber process.

d. Explain why the temperature chosen is a compromise temperature.

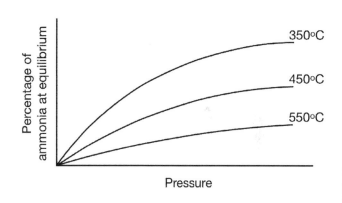

e. What is the role of the catalyst in the Haber process?

f. Explain why the Haber process should be carried out at a high pressure.

g. Explain why we do not carry out the reaction at a higher pressure than 200 atmospheres.

NPK Fertilisers

Exam tip: In question 2b below, you will calculate the percentage by mass of an element in a compound. This is not on the specification but has been in exam questions.

1. NPK fertilisers are used extensively in modern farming.

NPK fertilisers replace the elements taken in by plants when they grow.

a. Which elements are replaced by NPK fertilisers?

| Potassium | Sulfur | Nickel | Nitrogen | Phosphorus | Oxygen |

b. NPK fertilisers improve agricultural productivity. What does this mean?

c. Explain why NPK fertilisers are an example of a formulation.

2. The main compound of nitrogen in NPK fertilisers in ammonium nitrate.

Ammonium nitrate is made by reacting ammonia with nitric acid.

This is shown below.

| Ammonia | | Nitric acid | | Ammonium nitrate |

$$NH_3 \text{(g)} \quad + \quad HNO_3 \text{(aq)} \quad \longrightarrow \quad NH_4NO_3 \text{(aq)}$$

a. State the name of the process used to make the ammonia.

b. Calculate the percentage by mass of nitrogen in ammonium nitrate.

Use the equation on the right.

A_r N = 14, A_r H = 1, A_r O = 16

$$\% \text{ by mass} = \frac{\text{Mass of element in compound}}{\text{Relative formula mass of compound}} \times 100$$

c. Using your answer to question 2b, calculate the mass of nitrogen in 3000 g of ammonium nitrate.

3. The potassium in NPK fertilisers comes from the ground.

These compounds are either potassium chloride or potassium sulfate.

The charges of the ions involved are shown below.

Determine the formulas of potassium chloride and potassium sulfate.

Potassium chloride

Potassium sulfate

Potassium ion   Chloride ion   Sulfate ion

K^+ Cl^- SO_4^{2-}

4. The phosphate in NPK fertilisers comes in three different forms.

a. Complete the flowcharts below to show how these are made.

Method 1

Phosphate rock

React with Nitric acid

Calcium nitrate

React with ammonia

used in NPK fertiliser

Method 2

Phosphate rock

React with Sulfuric acid

Calcium sulfate

used in NPK fertiliser

Method 3

Phosphate rock

React with Phosphoric acid

used in NPK fertiliser

Exam tip: The specification states that you are expected to name the salts made when phosphate rock is reacted with nitric acid, sulfuric acid and phosphoric acid.

b. Suggest why the phosphoric acid made in method 1 cannot be used directly as a fertiliser.

c. Which of these reactions is more efficient in terms of energy and resources?

Explain your answer.

5. In the exam, you could be asked to compare the production of fertilisers in industry with their production in a school laboratory.

The flowcharts for these reactions are shown below.

a. Explain why dilute ammonia solution and dilute nitric acid are used in schools rather than ammonia gas and concentrated nitric acid.

b. Describe how the industrial production of ammonium nitrate is more energy efficient than that in a school laboratory.

c. Industrial production of ammonium nitrate is a continuous process whereas in a school it is a batch process.

Explain the advantage of a continuous process over a batch process.

Chemistry Paper 2

GCSE Specimen Paper

Time allowed: 105 minutes

Maximum marks: 100

Please note that this is a specimen exam paper written by freesciencelessons. The questions are meant to reflect the style of questions that you might see in your GCSE Chemistry exam.

Neither the exam paper nor the mark scheme have been endorsed by any exam board. The answers are my best estimates of what would be accepted but I cannot guarantee that this would be the case. I do not offer any guarantee that the level you achieve in this specimen paper is the level that you will achieve in the real exam.

1   This question is about the atmosphere today and in the past.

Figure 1 shows the gases in the atmosphere today.

Figure 1

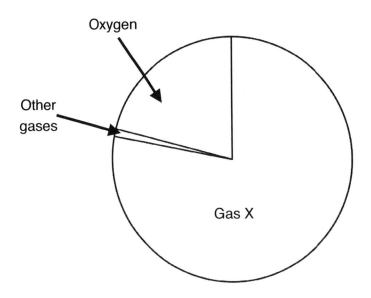

1 . 1   State the identity of gas X.

1 mark

_____

1 . 2   One of the other gases in the atmosphere is Argon which is found in group 0 of the periodic table.

What name do scientists give to group 0?

1 mark

_____

1 . 3   The Earth was formed around 4.6 billion years ago.

Complete the sentences below.

3 marks

Compared to the Earth today, the atmosphere of the early Earth contained a large

amount of water vapour and _____ . These

gases were released by _____ . When the Earth

cooled, the water vapour condensed to form the _____ .

1.4   Carbon dioxide is produced when humans burn fossil fuels such as methane.

Balance the equation below to show the combustion of methane.

1 mark

$$CH_4\text{(g)} + \_\_O_2\text{(g)} \longrightarrow CO_2\text{(g)} + \_\_H_2O\text{(l)}$$

1.5   Carbon dioxide is a greenhouse gas.

Describe how greenhouses gases cause the temperature of the atmosphere to increase.

3 marks

_____

_____

_____

_____

_____

_____

1.6   As well as carbon dioxide, burning fossil fuels can produce another oxide of carbon.

State the name of this chemical and describe how it is formed.

3 marks

_____

_____

_____

_____

Total = 12

2   Spices such as chilli powder often contain food colourings.

A scientist wanted to check that the colourings in chilli powder were safe to eat.

Her method is shown below.

1. Dissolve the chilli powder in a small amount of water.

2. Draw a pencil line 2cm from the bottom of a piece of chromatography paper.

3. Place a small spot of the chilli powder solution on the pencil line.

4. Place spots of safe food colourings on the pencil line.

5. Place the end of the chromatography paper into water.

6. Allow the water to run around ¾ to the top of the paper.

7. Mark the distance run by the water.

8. Allow the paper to dry.

2 . 1   Explain why the starting line is drawn in pencil and not pen ink.

1 mark

_____

_____

_____

2 . 2   In paper chromatography, state the mobile phase and the stationary phase.

2 marks

Mobile phase _____

_____

Stationary phase_____

_____

The scientist's results are shown in **figure 2**.

Figure 2

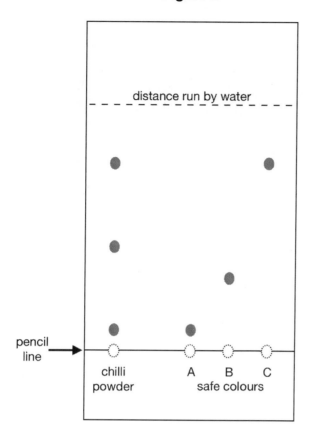

2 . 3   Explain why the colours in the chilli powder separated.

2 marks

_____

_____

_____

_____

2 . 4   Calculate the Rf value of safe colour C.

3 marks

Give your answer to 2 significant figures.

_____

_____

_____

Rf value = _____

2 . 5   State three conclusions about the chilli power which could be drawn from the results.

3 marks

_____

_____

_____

_____

_____

_____

2 . 6   Do the results prove that the chilli powder is safe to eat? Explain your answer.

2 marks

_____

_____

_____

_____

Total = 13

3   This question is about crude oil.

3.1   Crude oil is a mixture of hydrocarbons.

What is meant by a hydrocarbon?

2 marks

_____

_____

_____

3.2   Describe how crude oil is formed.

2 marks

_____

_____

_____

3.3   Butane is an alkane containing four carbon atoms.

Complete **figure 3** to show the structure of butane.

2 marks

Figure 3

C   C   C   C

3.4   Complete the sentences by selecting the correct words.

2 marks

Butane has a lower
| boiling point |
| flammability |
| viscosity |
than ethane.

Both ethane and butane have the general formula
| C_nH_{2n-2} |
| C_nH_{2n} |
| C_nH_{2n+2} |

3.5   Before they can be used, the hydrocarbons in crude oil must be separated.

Describe how the hydrocarbons in crude oil are separated.

5 marks

_____

_____

_____

_____

_____

_____

_____

_____

3.6   Long chain hydrocarbons can be cracked to produce shorter chain hydrocarbons.

Complete the cracking equation below.

1 mark

$$C_{10}H_{22} \xrightarrow[\text{high temperature}]{\text{catalyst}} C_2H_4 \quad + \quad \underline{\hspace{4cm}}$$

3.7   During cracking, an alkene is produced.

Describe how we can test for alkenes.

2 marks

_____

_____

_____

Total = 16

4   This question is about metals.

4.1   Metals are a finite resource.

1 mark

Explain what is meant by a finite resource.

_____

_____

_____

4.2   Copper can be extracted from copper oxide by heating with carbon.

The equation for this is shown below.

$$2\ CuO \quad + \quad C \quad \longrightarrow \quad 2\ Cu \quad + \quad CO_2$$

Calculate the maximum mass of copper that could be extracted from 318 g of copper oxide.

3 marks

$A_r\ Cu = 63.5,\ A_r\ O = 16,\ A_r\ C = 12$

_____

_____

_____

_____

_____

Maximum mass of copper = _____ g

4.3   Metals such as copper can also be extracted by alternative methods.

These include phytomining.

Explain how phytomining is carried out.

3 marks

_____

_____

_____

_____

4.4   Copper can be combined with tin to form the alloy bronze.

Bronze is harder than pure copper.

Explain why alloys are harder than pure metals.

2 marks

_____

_____

_____

Total = 9

5   This question is about water.

In the UK, potable water is produced from fresh water, for example from rivers or lakes.

The stages of producing potable water are outlined in **figure 4**.

Figure 4

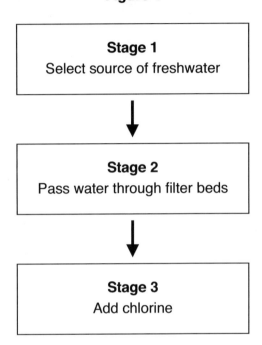

Stage 1
Select source of freshwater

Stage 2
Pass water through filter beds

Stage 3
Add chlorine

5 . 1   Describe what is meant by potable water.

1 mark

_____

_____

5 . 2   State the purpose of stage 3.

1 mark

_____

_____

5.3 Potable water can also be made from desalination of sea water.

Name a method for carrying out desalination.

1 mark

_____

_____

5.4 Describe a disadvantage of making potable water by desalination.

1 mark

_____

_____

5.5 Pure water contains no dissolved solids.

Describe how a student could check to see if a sample of water contained no dissolved solids.

4 marks

_____

_____

_____

_____

_____

_____

_____

5.6   A student found a bottle labelled "copper sulfate solution".

Describe how the student could test the solution to determine that it contained copper ions and sulfate ions.

In both cases, state what would be observed if the result was positive.

Test for copper ions

2 marks

_____

_____

_____

_____

Test for sulfate ions

3 marks

_____

_____

_____

_____

Total = 13

6   Calcium carbonate reacts with hydrochloric acid.

The equation for this reaction is

Calcium   +   Hydrochloric   ⟶   Calcium   +   Carbon   +   Water
carbonate   acid   chloride   Dioxide

A student wanted to measure the rate of the reaction shown above.

The student used excess calcium carbonate.

The apparatus they used is shown in **figure 5**.

Figure 5

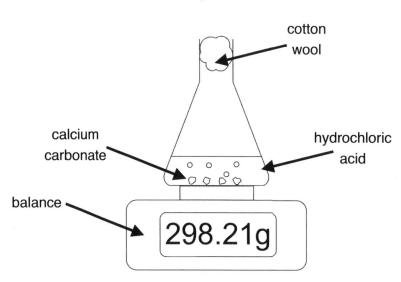

6 . 1   State the resolution of the balance.

1 mark

_____

_____

6 . 2   Describe the function of the cotton wool.

2 marks

_____

_____

_____

The student's results are shown in **table 1**.

Table 1

Time in seconds	Mass of carbon dioxide released in grams
0	0.00
10	0.32
20	0.60
30	0.76
40	0.86
50	0.92
60	0.92

6 . 3   Plot the student's results on **figure 6**.

Draw a line of best fit.

3 marks

Figure 6

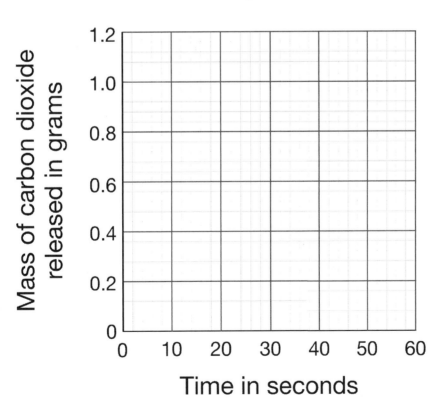

6 . 4   Using the graph, state the time that the reaction stopped.

1 mark

_____

_____

6 . 5   Explain why the reaction stopped.

1 mark

_____

_____

6 . 6   Use the graph to determine the mean rate of reaction at 25 seconds.

3 marks

Mean rate of reaction at 25 seconds = _____

6 . 7   The student repeated the experiment using smaller pieces of calcium carbonate.

Draw a new line on **figure 6** to show how the mass of carbon dioxide released changes with time.

2 marks

6 . 8   State a control variable in this experiment.

1 mark

_____

_____

Total = 14

7 Ethanol can be made by reacting ethene with steam.

The equation for this reaction is shown below.

$$C_2H_4 \text{ (g)} \quad + \quad H_2O \text{ ( )} \quad \rightleftharpoons \quad CH_3CH_2OH \text{ (g)}$$

7.1 Give the name of this type of reaction.

1 mark

_____

7.2 Complete the equation by inserting the correct state symbol into the space.

1 mark

7.3 Ethanol can also be produced from sugars by fermentation.

Describe how fermentation is carried out.

3 marks

_____

_____

_____

_____

7.4 Producing ethanol by fermentation is more sustainable than by using ethene.

Suggest two reasons why.

2 marks

_____

_____

_____

_____

7.5   Ethanol reacts with sodium. The equation for this is shown below.

Ethanol   +   Sodium   ⟶   Sodium ethoxide   +   _____

Complete the equation to show the second product.

1 mark

7.6   Ethanol can be reacted to produce ethanoic acid.

Ethanoic acid is a carboxylic acid.

Complete the diagram below to show the structure of ethanoic acid.

1 mark

```
    H
    |
H − C
    |
    H
```

7.7   Explain why carboxylic acids are weak acids.

2 marks

_____

_____

7.8   Complete the sentence below.

At the same concentration, carboxylic acids have a _____ pH

than strong acids.

1 mark

7.9   Ethanoic acid and ethanol react to produce ethyl ethanoate.

What type of molecule is ethyl ethanoate?

1 mark

_____

Total = 13

8   Poly(propene) is a polymer made from propene.

Propene is an alkene.

8 . 1   What name is given to the small molecules such as propene which are used to make a polymer?

1 mark

8 . 2   The structure of a small section of poly(propene) is shown in **figure 7**.

Figure 7

Draw the repeating unit for poly(propene) in the space below.

3 marks

8 . 3   State the type of polymerisation which is used to make polymers such as poly(propene).

1 mark

Polymers can be thermosoftening or thermosetting.

Figure 8 shows the structures of thermosoftening and thermosetting polymers.

Figure 8

Thermosoftening
polymer

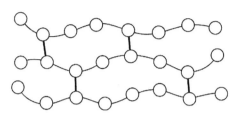

Thermosetting
polymer

8.4   Describe and explain the properties of thermosoftening and thermosetting polymers.

4 marks

Thermosoftening polymers _____

_____

_____

_____

Thermosetting polymers _____

_____

_____

_____

8.5   Fibreglass contains glass fibres embedded in a polymer resin.

What name do scientists give to materials such as fibreglass?

1 mark

_____

Total = 10

Printed in Great Britain
by Amazon